6029

THE
SUPER
YEARS

THE SUPER YEARS

Charlotte Hale

Fleming H. Revell Company
Old Tappan, New Jersey

Scripture quotations in this volume are from the King James Version of the Bible.

Excerpts from THE DELIGHTS OF GROWING OLD by Maurice Goudeket reprinted by permission of Farrar, Straus and Giroux, Inc. Translated from the French by Patrick O'Brien. Copyright © 1966 by Farrar, Straus and Giroux, Inc.

Excerpts from SIXTY-PLUS & FIT AGAIN by Magda Rosenberg. Copyright © 1977 by Magda Rosenberg. Reprinted by permission of the publisher, M. Evans and Co., Inc., New York, New York 10017.

Quotes by Grandma Moses from her autobiography, *My Life's History.* Copyright © 1952, Grandma Moses Properties Co., New York.

Excerpt from THE NEW AEROBICS by Kenneth H. Cooper, M.D. Copyright © 1970 by Kenneth H. Cooper. Reprinted by permission of the publisher, M. Evans and Company, Inc., New York, New York 10017.

Excerpts from *Albert Schweitzer's Gift of Friendship* by Erica Anderson copyright © 1964 by Erica Anderson. Permission granted by Roslyn Targ Literary Agency.

Library of Congress Cataloging in Publication Data

Hale, Charlotte.
    The super years.

    1. Aged—United States—Psychology.   2. Old age—
Psychological aspects.   3. Mental health.   4. Success.
5. Happiness.   I. Title.
HQ1064.U5H19   1984   305.2'6   83-19224
ISBN 0-8007-1349-4

For Eleanor Cunningham Hale,
my mother,
who taught me to love words and books;
and in memory of Anthony Winston Hale,
my father,
who taught me to love life

Contents

Foreword

Nᴏᴛ ᴏꜰᴛᴇɴ, I imagine, does one get the opportunity to write a book that's so much fun, you wish it were possible to begin all over again!

That's the way it is with *Super Years*, which will surprise a few friends who politely inquired as to what I was writing then. I could only answer—lamely—"Oh-h-h, a book on aging. Or *not* aging, depending on how you look at it."

"Oh?" they'd say, the nonenthusiasm rolling out before us like a large, flat rug. Sorry, friends, but how do you convey that you've somehow stumbled onto one of the most exciting subjects of your career—a book so fresh and surprising, so tremendously nonstereotyped, that if you talked about it at all, you'd only gush?

Well, I've become a gusher. For one thing, *aging* wasn't it at all. Soon into the flight, I perceived that the book really covers *attitudes*. You can't pin these people down at all, agewise. What can you say about a ninety-two-year-old beauty who works regularly as a fashion model? Or how do you cover the eighty-four-year-old sportsman, enthusiastic about his new exercise trampoline, since it helps him improve his parachute jumps? (The difficulty, of course, being the challenge of finding the exercise program which properly accommodates itself to his artificial leg.)

Quite simply, researching and writing this book greatly altered

my already positive outlook on life. Originally, my aim had been
to find and interview older Americans who could give real insights into their successful latter years. How naive! For one thing,
I didn't realize that nearly half the population of the USA has
somehow grown up and reached aged fifty or older. Soon, highly
successful older Americans seemed to pop out at me from behind every bush. There are millions—literally—and now I began to observe them smiling forth from television and magazine
advertisements.

"Old age is *in!*" I exulted. "And here I am, preparing to
ride the crest of the wave. How wonderful that I'll soon be old
enough . . ."

Surveying today's ads, you just want to hurry up and get there.
See the handsome grandpas, tanned and unwrinkled, with nary a
little tummy hanging over a belt. Magazine "grands," tall and
broad-shouldered almost to a fault, cast crinkle-eyed smiles towards new-wave grandmas who could still wear the straight skirts
they took to college.

White hair is back in style, I also observe. The ladies emerging
from sleek new-model automobiles have it, as do belles in shampoo advertisements. I noted that white hair looks even better with
one's emeralds or sapphires for contrast, which is probably why
the ad ladies wear those knockout earrings.

You know, of course, I wasn't just captivated by such superfi-
cial changes. Rather, the whole beautiful spectrum—everything
from counseling for one's second, third, or even *fourth* career, to
exercise classes for people seventy and above—I had known
nothing about.

Stories about eighty-year-old pilots, mountain climbers or
water skiers abound. Volunteerism flourishes too, in this age

group; surrogate grandparents, volunteer law enforcers, drug counselors, firemen, small-business advisors, librarians . . .

Particularly inspiring, too, are the infinite number of ways retirees, even those approaching the century mark, serve and give to others. Two women, one a privileged community leader, the other her household helper of fifty years, regularly receive donations of well-kept baby clothes. Together they launder and tenderly press the tiny ruffled garments, creating perfectly fresh layettes for needy lambs. During the past half-century, employer and servant have clothed hundreds and hundreds of infants.

Atlanta's Saint James United Methodist Church began a dynamic food project, thanks to five men and one woman, all retired, who work fifteen terraced beds in a 720-square-foot vegetable garden near the church's activities building. The garden produces hundreds of pounds of pole beans, squash, okra, cucumbers, tomatoes, swiss chard, and lima beans, which are donated to the community kitchen operated by Saint Luke's Episcopal Church in downtown Atlanta.

Community to community, denomination to denomination, person to person—how the fellowship, the inspired cooperation, the openhearted service does grow!

These days the arts receive booster shots as "new" older artists enter the ranks. People fifty and above actually can learn to play the piano with more skill than their grandkids, due to mature discipline and determination to succeed, reports a neurologist who tried it—successfully.

Then there's the sixty-five-year-old grandmother who decides to write a best-seller, and does. "Of course," she shrugged, "I never could have written a book that good before now: I would have been too young and inexperienced."

The beloved Maria von Trapp learned to ride horseback and to snow ski at age sixty-four, she reports in her autobiography. After all, it would be a shame to have a beautiful Vermont ski lodge and never get to ski!

Most touching of all, to me, were dozens of reports of how old people had modeled behavior and attitudes that today's achievers eventually copied. Again and again I heard about grandparents, aged schoolteachers, ministers, or even movie stars who had inspired their middle-aged followers to go for it. I know something about that, too: Had my young mother not married a middle-aged man, I wouldn't be here.

Having acquired a fifty-seven-year-old father at my birth, I always knew the benefits and sang the praises of older men. Except for a few minor flaws (I hear they spoil their children rotten, though my siblings and I would never agree to that) a white-haired father makes the very finest kind of father.

He's already broken in. He wastes no time debating about trivia, such as no lollipops before lunch or hopscotch just before bedtime. He doesn't fear it will stunt your growth if you wake up at midnight to see the shooting stars, or even just to sneak a piece of mincemeat pie.

Prejudices like that, I dare say, helped me to choose some very mature friends. At age seven, I adored Miss Nina, who was still teaching school in her seventies. Nor can I forget Miss Libbie and Miss Mellie, who wore high, boned-lace collars around their wrinkled throats and spoke in little crystal voices. Mr. Howard, our white-haired Sunday-school superintendent, became my forever-friend after I won first prize in his essay contest on "My Favorite Beatitude."

Why so many old, old friends? I thought they knew so much more than other people! Also, I remembered, I loved them because they loved me. They gave me stories, paper-doll books, crisp cookies, and gentle advice. I watered their flowers, showed them my "poems," played their pianos, confided in them my dreams.

Years later came my first book, written with Miss Layona Glenn, an amazing and outrageous national treasure at age 103! Our taped interviews took me forever to transcribe, because she was so funny. We spent entirely too much interview time on jokes, laughter, and giggles.

Life comes full circle from time to time. Long before *The Super Years,* Miss Mellie, Mr. Howard, and so many other neighbors, teachers, and assorted elderly darlings *demonstrated* to me what it's really all about.

No wonder I gravitated to the subject. Hundreds of sugar cookies, watermelon cuttings, bee stings, what-I'm-going-to-be-when-I-grow-ups later, it dawns on me, I was *born* into the Super Years, and I shall inherit them.

So will you. You had your Miss Nina, as I had mine. Now, delightfully, our nation has produced a bumper crop of beauty, wisdom, intelligence and spunk, as demonstrated by millions of citizens in the upper-age groups.

How fortunate we are! May God bless each one.

CHARLOTTE HALE

THE
SUPER
YEARS

CHAPTER 1

The Super Years

WHAT'S ahead for you? The Super Years!

Super Years! They're the astonishing, lengthening chain of days, months, seasons and anniversaries—perhaps never expected or imagined—so wondrously extending healthy lives these days.

Americans are living longer. It's "in" to be older. Soon half our population will be fabulously fifty and above, with no pretense at holding. Our national life expectancy rate steadily climbs. Paradoxically, however, even as we find our *lives* lengthening, our *attitudes* about aging can stay shortsighted, stuffy, and out of style.

Example: It's *great* to live longer; it's *terrible* to be older. Thus we all help give Old Age a bad press. Super Years? For most of us, the post-fifty picture doesn't pop up in our minds as "Super": *Diseased, Disowned* and *Distressed* would be more like it! At best, we'd label Old Age as "Dullsville"—and we're dead wrong.

For the tremendous majority of us, current reports about Middle Age, Old Age and Old, Old, Old Age absolutely ring with promise. *The Super Years*—it's no misnomer. As additional facts about aging pour in, the news could hardly sound happier. Americans fifty years old and above appear demonstrably healthy, happy, and handsome. Look around. Everywhere—

starting, no doubt, within your own mirror—you see living proof. Clearly we're doing many good things for our bodies—but our *minds* may need a color rinse!

Take a look at your own post-fifty life-style. Hate that gray? Rethink it away! Unless you're already living life to the maximum, with every intention to continue that way, I hope this book challenges you to rethink. Your Super Years should become vivid and bountiful, as these statements show:

• America's average life expectancy has zoomed into the high 70s for women and 69 for men and continues to climb. By the year 2000 some researchers believe age 100 will be the national norm.

• Latest census figures report there are 32,000 Americans over 100. The second-fastest-growing age group in America is the over-85 group, which totals 2.4 million.

• Longevity studies report stunning *advances against aging,* including belief that it can be avoided or reversed.

• You can become *medically younger* at any point in your life. Men and women who appear twenty years younger than their chronological age actually look the way we're supposed to look!

Your Super Years should offer quantity *and* quality.

Super means ideal, first-rate. Super Years are to be enjoyed in good health, with optimum vigor. Your added years can brim with the best of the best. You can continue to learn, love, grow, experience, experiment, decide and change—*indefinitely.*

Super Years are yours when you:

1. Get your life together, then tie it with red ribbons.

2. Not only think, you *know.*

3. Love a lot.

4. Begin to laugh a lot more.

5. Decide to go for it.

6. Gladly change horses in midstream.

7. Come to the party!

Your Super Years are for deciding: Shall I slow down or skip? Wander or waltz? Stutter or sing? Knit or ski? Stay or go?

How about late marriage? A new career? Studying music? Learning Chinese? Writing a book? Hiking the Appalachian Trail? Your options are endless—and marvelous.

What about *your* sixties? Seventies? Eighties? Nineties and beyond? "Life turns out to be much longer than you think. It would pay to plan better," one man told me. And so it would. What would you do with three "extra" Aprils? Or another twelve Christmases? Or even one glorious, added autumn?

You were built to last. Indeed, you almost certainly were designed to live much longer and better than you've planned for. Think about it. *Everything about you* was designed to favor healing, recovery, endurance, survival—even regeneration. Presently some researchers believe healthy humans should live at least one century; others say 120 years; and at least one study reports our minds and bodies could function, with proper care, for a century and a half.

Obviously our thinking must do an about-face. We must choose not to grow "old" as we know it, with every ugly and defeating connotation that phrase currently implies. We must decide to *live* those Super Years. They can—and should—prove magnificently valuable, the best and most beautiful years of our lives.

You might visualize your life as a cornucopia, a horn of plenty. Look backward, and you see only the obscure, narrow beginning of the horn. Face forward, however, and you can picture the cornucopia opening outward—wide, brimming, gift-producing, overflowing, abundant life. Yes, there's *plenty* in store for you!

Some super facts—along with startling new beliefs about aging—rise like cream atop reports released by some fifty public, private, university and government-sponsored longevity centers. Coincidentally, as Americans reach sixty-five, that old magic vocational cutoff point, fewer and fewer of us actually retire. Old attitudes toward health, mental capacity, social usefulness, productivity, and sexual capacity are changing—not so much because people are changing as because of increased knowledge about life in our seventies, eighties, and beyond.

As new data accumulates and breakthroughs develop, exciting prospects for full-faceted later life whirl into view. You and I stand an excellent chance of enjoying some of the most fruitful latter-life experiences known to mankind.

Despite widespread reports concerning illness, nursing homes, unemployed, and unwanted oldsters, the fact is that only 5 percent of those above age 65 become helpless and dependent. The overwhelming majority of us can expect to enjoy happy, healthy futures—productive and important years, if we so choose.

Your Super Years dance ahead of you. What is Middle Age these days? When does Old Age begin? Distinctions are becoming increasingly blurred, it seems—and it's high time. Wherever you stand on the age continuum at this moment, you can take a rich, exciting treasure of personal resources into your Super Years.

As Victor Hugo exulted, "Winter is on my head, but eternal spring is in my heart." Begin to distill all you've gathered so far about living, loving, and learning—and it's magnificently so!

Right now, consider your next three decades. Do you anticipate pain or payoff? Loving or losing? Learning or quitting? Shrinking or expanding? Whatever your views, today you can begin to see your life in terms of Super Years. As you read this book, imagine yourself increasingly in these ways:

• **Your Brainpower.** Continuous learning does it. Your brain orders up the menu of your life, and *you* decide how bland or spicy to make it. Decisions, emotions, and motor skills; thinking, speaking, and acting; simple or complex, everything you do begins in your brain. At any time of life, you can increase your brain power.

• **Your Social Life.** Decide to enlarge it, refine it, value it. As the Girl Scout round goes, "Make new friends, but keep the old; One is silver, the other is gold." Today is the day to choose and cherish those friends who'll enhance the rest of your life.

• **Travel.** More than four out of five persons beyond age 65 keep themselves fully mobile. Most remain as active and adventurous as their younger neighbors. People above age 65, for example, take nearly one-third of our nation's automobile trips. You can continue to go far! Time, strength, money, and desire for travel can be yours.

• **Your Environment.** Your eyes, heart, and spirit forever will warm to beauty, so why not plan for it? Begin to dream. Ask yourself, what do I want and need in my Super Years? How do I see my office? My kitchen? My studio? Bring enthusiasm to your project, as you mentally tailor your surroundings to your continually developing Self. The benefits? Enormous!

- **Your Physical Fitness.** No matter where you stand on the age or fitness scale, if you're basically healthy, you can begin today to reverse the effects of yesterday's laxity or body abuse. Overweight or stress; alcohol, tobacco, and drug use; sedentary life-style; chronic disease; these and other *negatives* can be traded at any age for a beneficial set of *positives*. You can help your body become medically younger. This book can show you how to begin.

- **Good Looks.** Most of us have far better looks than we bother to use. We could improve our appearance; some of us, dramatically. Smarter clothing, color analysis, improved posture and muscle tone, better grooming, attention to style, plastic surgery or face-lifts, dental restoration, can work miracles. This book will stimulate you to plan ahead to enhance your beauty and good looks. They should last for the rest of your life!

- **Your Activities.** More than one-fourth of all retired persons decide to return to full or part-time employment. Many start their first personal businesses. Many others change careers. For some it's time to explore the arts, develop long-dormant talents, become "new persons."

Your Super Years will coincide with the current growing demand for older people's talents. Corporate officers hire retirees as consultants. Business, civic, church and charity organizations seek older citizens for sensitive volunteer or paid positions. We'll explore some possibilities in a later chapter. You're valuable, and everybody else has begun to know it!

• **Your Independence.** Despite a generalized fear of aging and monetary dependency, facts often prove vastly different from what we imagine. Nearly three-quarters of all Americans beyond age 65 own their own homes or have small mortgages. That same group had a combined income of $163 billion in 1978 (the last year for which figures are available). That per-person average exceeds figures for those aged 35 to 44, or 18 to 25.

Surprised? The fact is, persons aged 55 to 64 presently rank per capita as the most affluent group in America. Start to think how you'll retain your independence.

Super Years! As you read this book, begin to research your own best ways to make them happen. You might begin by examining the following ten ideas:

1. You can succeed *not in spite of old age, but because of it.*

2. There's no such stage as "too old" (or "too young").

3. Don't quit while you're alive.

4. You can live several lives in one lifetime, if you choose.

5. All things come to those who *don't* wait.

6. You're never too old to grow up—and out.

7. If you lose one skill or ability, find others to replace it.

8. Nobody, but *nobody,* ever outgrows a need for love.

9. Learning, working, living skills are like good scissors—they sharpen with use.

10. There's always something great about to happen.

Decide to become more alert to those who already have lived long enough to prove such statements. For example, I thrilled to Maurice Goudeket's romantic autobiography entitled *The Delights of Growing Old.* "There is no happier condition than that of an aged man," he audaciously states. "To begin with, let me—I who shall be seventy-five before this book is finished—tell you a secret: it is not really a fact that you grow old at all."

Monsieur Goudeket's "secret" ties in with researchers' growing respect for the role your brain plays in your life. "The brain is you. It is human personality. It changes all through your life, and it changes your life in turn," said Dr. Arnold S. Scheibel, a UCLA brain researcher.

"It is possible for an eighty-year-old to have a thirty-year-old brain," the neuropsychiatrist said. The secret? Simply use!

"We hope to show that a brain kept young by use will keep the body younger longer," he added. "We know the brain talks to the body all the time. . . . So if the thinking, feeling, emotional brain is going to change bodily aging, it will be the hypothalamus where it happens."

What controls your thinking? What sort of brain work will engage your Super Years? What has determined your attitudes toward aging—particularly your own old age?

"As a man thinketh, so is he," King Solomon wrote. (*See* Proverbs 23:7.) Who taught you what your latter years should contain? Doctors? Family history? The media? Did aging friends and family members shape your viewpoint? Also, ask yourself, At what point do I consider a person to be "over the hill"?

Such mind-sets point us into our Super Years. Change your thinking today, and you'll change the course of your life. "The mind can be a healer or a slayer," wrote Angela Fox Dunn in the *Los Angeles Times.* "How long we live—and how well we age—

is something we, each of us, can help to determine."

David Trumble, an "ordinary" citizen of Cannifton, Ontario, well illustrates her contention. At 114, Mr. Trumble walks 8 miles a day and still loves to dance! At age 8, he began working in a lumber camp. He engaged in hard farm labor until he retired at age 96; quit smoking at 100; drove a car until he was 104, wrote by dictation and published a book at 109, a second book at 111, and is working on his third book as this is written.

"Life is meant for living," David Trumble told a *National Enquirer* reporter. "I've lived this long because God has kept me alive. I'm not going until He takes me and when He does, I'll be ready. I can't complain. I've lived a good life."

Like Maurice Goudeket, Mr. Trumble knows a secret: you really don't have to grow old. Are people like him remarkable? Not really. Unusual? Hardly. These and other Super Years celebrants you'll meet in this book illustrate a belief held by James Maas, 62, an anthropologist who works with the San Francisco Police Department—that people who age successfully are in the majority.

Really, it makes sense. Life lived at daily capacity, by age 70 or so, should produce enormous cumulative effects in even very "ordinary" lives. Expansion, not reduction, must be our Creator's divine intention for us. We're built so as to flourish and succeed. We're created for those magnificent Super Years!

Napoleon Hill, author of *Think and Grow Rich,* once stated that the average age for attaining millionaire status is in the sixties. Obviously, accumulated wisdom, experience, patience, and other gifts eventually should yield a superior level of productive effect. That raises a major question: Do most of us shut down our lives far short of earning real success—or just prior to it?

Your Super Years can contain significant levels of fulfillment and success. Ask yourself, *What do I want to be when I grow up?* (Ask yourself even if you're 99!) Will I, like Abraham, receive God's promise when I am 90? Will I, like Sarah, still be physically beautiful when I'm 90? Like Moses, could I become a successful leader of men—at 80?

Do I expect my old age to be as life-changing, as historically important, as that of industrialist F. Buckminster Fuller? John Wesley? Dr. Albert Schweitzer? Benjamin Franklin? Dr. B. F. Skinner? Mother Theresa?

Clearly, the choice is up to us. This admonition was set forth for us many centuries ago: ". . . I have set before you life and death, blessing and cursing: therefore choose life, that both thou and thy seed may live" (Deuteronomy 30:19).

We make such choices daily. A journalist tells of approaching Mahatma Gandhi, who led the masses in India to achieve national independence, on his seventy-eighth birthday. He asked that beloved figure if his birthday had roused any thoughts he might like to share with the world.

"Oh, is this my birthday?" Gandhi asked, surprised. "I did not know. Every day is my birthday."

If every day is *your* birthday, you can expect a lifetime of Super Years. You'll choose to face forward. Your latter years will bless others as well as yourself. You're learning each day how to love, and how to give. You're learning to expect and receive the love of God and man.

Because you choose life—abundant life—you're well acquainted with the challenge, growth, and sheer fun each year provides. You know your Super Years will spring forth from your own lively answers to life's questions.

You own a wonderful calendar. On this, you can record the

data vitally important to every day of your life. The calendar? Of course, it's your *brain*.

Your brain can keep you young. Your brain can choose—and literally program you for—your Super Years!

CHAPTER 2

Out of Your Mind

How is your love life?

That depends, of course, on your brain! Everything about you comes out of your mind. Not only do feelings of love, caring, and desire originate in your brain, but everything else about you as well: your health, emotions, habits, occupations, skills, interests, happiness and all the rest.

Your brain can prolong your youth or reverse your age. Researchers say *using* the brain staves off the aging process. At any age, you can retrain your mind by means of stimulus, environment, education, reading, music, math, art, people, travel, ideas and a host of other approaches.

Quite simply, your brain can design and execute your Super Years! Paul Neimark, writing in *Success* magazine, explains it this way: "No, it isn't the late, late show. For us, it is the early, *early* show.

"But, as with success in *anything,* you must have a positive attitude. The thoughts we accept into the organ we call the brain are the final ingredient of staying young.

"This means more—much more—than mere 'positive thinking.' It means knowing that you *can* do it, knowing *how* to do it, and *wanting* to do it."

According to writer Angela Fox Dunn, we must challenge our

capacities. "As old as you think? It's really true!" she says. Dunn writes that if we keep challenging our mental and emotional capacities—"Learn a new skill, study a new subject, take up tennis, fall in love!"—we have a much better chance of staying younger longer.

The irrepressible Satchel Paige once said, "Age is nothing but mind over matter. If you don't mind, it don't matter!" He'd doubtless chuckle to learn that scientists today burn their lamps late, proving his thesis correct.

Your brain not only determines your rate of aging, it also controls the rest of your Self. And what a complex Self! "Bucky" Fuller, inventor of the geodesic dome and at 87 still considered the consummate scientist, inventor, philosopher, and problem-solver, described himself (and us) in engineering terms:

A self-balancing, twenty-eight joined, adapter base biped; an electro-chemical reduction plant, integrated with segregated stowages and thousands of hydraulic and pneumatic pumps with motors attached, 62,000 miles of capillaries, millions of warning signals . . . guided with exquisite precision from a turret in which are located telescopic and microscopic self-registering and recording range-finders. . . .

No wonder he confidently continued his own breakneck work schedule so late into life. Fuller described a human being as "basically a pattern in integrity" that is *indestructible.* "You and I are essential functions of the universe," he pronounced. "I'll be seeing you. Forever!"

The Super Years, then, aren't accidental. They're the product of thinking, feeling, planning, hoping, *living* men and women—all of them vital, certainly, but many not the sort you'd necessarily label "brainy." The retired, passive, sedentary Ph.D., for example, might age far more rapidly than a grocery clerk who grows a garden, teaches Sunday school, repairs his own car, and sings in the community chorus.

Think of the "oldest" and most interesting individuals you know—those who actively demonstrate their Super Years. No doubt they kick up their heels to the point it worries their dull, gray, middle-aged "kids." Jot each name on a piece of paper: your 89-year-old grandmother, perhaps, or Old Man Corrigan, who's past 90 and still climbs mountains. Beneath each name, list the activities in which these people still engage: cooking, gardening, laundry, tax returns, reading, church work, driving a car, whatever else you know they do.

Now study the lists. Phenomenal! Notice the breadth of interests, the range of skills each one still possesses. How do your own present activities compare? What things will you know how to do for fun and profit when you're 80, 90, or 100? Remember, your Super Years begin now. They begin in your head. They come out of your mind, your thought, and your muscles.

As you think about Grandma, or Old Man Corrigan, notice that individuals who age well—which is to say, who *ignore* age— invariably seem comfortable with themselves. They set their own goals, maintain a high sense of purpose, and know how to live in day-tight compartments. But above all, they do their own thinking! You can learn how to live that same beautifully rhythmic, apparently effortless life-style. It comes out of your mind!

Plan plenty of variety, which spices life, as you dream up the menu for *your* Super Years. A balanced life—one that nourishes your mind, body, and spirit—yields longer, richer living. Still, how few of us feed all three elements of our Selves equally well. If we're intellectual, it's easy to neglect the spiritual; and if we're spiritually well-nourished, what about our physical selves?

Others spend years developing that balanced life-style to a high art. They age brilliantly. At age 70, Benjamin Franklin—printer, inventor, scientist, journalist, statesman, and a framer of the United States Constitution—approached the height of his powers. Despite ill health, summer 1775 to summer 1776 became the busiest year of his life. Imagine a typical day in the life of Benjamin Franklin, as described by his biographer, Verner W. Crane:

> Up at dawn supervising the training of the Pennsylvania militia, planning arms dumps and caches, scouting out sources of saltpeter, studying various chemical formulae for gunpowder.
>
> The committee asked him to design a new model of pike for infantry use against a British bayonet charge. He helped design a river obstruction of iron and logs on the model of the French chevaux de frise. Placed in the channel leading to the harbor, these obstructions later kept the British fleet out of range of Philadephia for almost two months.
>
> Franklin went out little, went to bed early to prepare for a day that would exhaust any man, let alone one moving into his seventieth year.

In September 1775, with the American Revolution raging, Franklin found himself "immersed in so much business that I have scarce time to eat or sleep." Always the soul of prudence and moderation, Franklin disapproved of wartime excesses. "This bustle," he wrote, "is unsuitable to age."

Unsuitable or not, Benjamin Franklin worked tirelessly toward the formation of our republic until just before his death at 84. His life exemplified the power in balanced living, in developing an incredibly broad range of interests and abilities. Benjamin Franklin worked and learned *all his life.* He excelled at more jobs than most people ever dream of tackling!

If *using* the brain and balancing its activities retards aging, Dr. Albert Schweitzer's renowned work in Africa will illustrate that point. Erica Anderson, photographer and biographer, marveled at the 90-year-old Schweitzer's ability to work for long hours in his clinic, then take up his labors again in the evening. Not only as a physician, the biographer observed, but also as philosopher, preacher, musician, and servant, Dr. Schweitzer still exhibited amazing, youthful energy. She watched him, and she wrote in *Albert Schweitzer's Gift of Friendship:*

> ... the secret of his vitality is the frequency with which he shifts from one activity to another. When he's tired of writing, he goes out and works in the hot sun, building. When his feet are dragging from outdoor labor, he changes into his organ shoes and practices at the piano. When fatigue strikes him there, he returns to some desk work. Employing this rotating schedule, he's continually refreshed, instead of tired, by each new activity.

Out of your *mind!* That's where your youthful outlook or your aging Self originates. In *Success Can Be Yours,* Mack R. Douglas gives us Dr. Flanders Dunbar's prescription for long life:

1. Good health habits.

2. Marriage. (Ninety-eight percent of the 80-year-old doctors are married.)

3. Large families.

4. Ingenuity in avoiding frustration.

5. Not worrying about getting to the top.

6. Sociability and sense of humor.

7. Not worrying about things beyond your control.

8. Ability to sleep soundly.

9. Ability to make a fresh start.

10. No fear of death.

11. Religious conviction.

There you have it—one super recipe for your Super Years, all dependent on good mind control. Activate your brain. Begin today. Your ability to learn and love, do and become, will add years to your life and life to your years!

Good brain use, of course, demands that you instruct your mind to begin pulling the weeds from your garden of thoughts. As the computer slogan puts it, GARBAGE IN, GARBAGE OUT. If we continually "compute" a load of negatives, we can only look ahead to Sorry Years. Most of us harbor a few unconscious negative traits, of course, but we can *decide* to change.

The negatives of life effectively cut off the flow. Worry, pessimism, lack of faith; boredom and resentment; self-pity, gossip and fear; these and other such dreary items need to go. Your mind is in control. Your brain can decide exactly when and how to do the weeding (more about this in the chapters ahead) and how to replace those unwanted roots with rare, flowering traits of character.

An attorney described how his mother programmed her own brain, resulting in her extraordinarily happy and effective long life. "She has lived by the Scripture [Philippians 4:8] . . . 'whatsoever things are just, whatsoever things are pure, whatsoever things are lovely, whatsoever things are of good report . . . think on these things.'

"As a result, at age ninety-four, nothing but goodness comes from my mother's mouth," the son explained.

What a powerful truth! At any age, you can decide to train your mind for good. You can dig out all negatives by the roots. You can substitute energizing, life-changing positives *today*.

While you're at it, why not haul away some of your "old thinking" ideas, too? They're just lying there like soggy, old logs! Dated opinions, resistance to new thoughts, hatred for topical music, books, or entertainment—this sort of mind-set keeps your feet planted firmly in vanished decades.

Why not allow your brain to explore, taste, think, or at least be *somewhat* exposed to things current? Should you reject today's and tomorrow's ideas, still your mind deserves a chance at them. Like any muscle, the more your mind works, the more it *can* work. Exercise your brain. Keep it supple and flexible. You'll enjoy it throughout your Super Years!

Brain work. Take your mind off automatic pilot and let it zoom. Your brain, now or later—even much, much later—is designed to take your thoughts, habits, and desires anywhere you'd like them to go.

Scientists claim that during our lifetime each of us uses less than 10 percent of our mental potential. Even so, the human brain has conceived the laser beam, poetry, computers, space exploration, and symphonic music. The brain directs physical exploits, prayer, and acts of mercy. The brain guides throughout relationships; difficult studies; automatic tasks; and wondrous loves.

Your mind will create, direct, and stimulate your Super Years.

Those special seasons will contain exactly the elements *your* brain can conceive, believe, and receive—*and nothing more.*

As Maurice Goudeket wrote:

Everybody agrees that it is necessary to make one's body obey rules of hygiene; but not everybody asks whether there may not also be rules of mental hygiene. A man who devotes three quarters of an hour every morning to physical jerks, which he usually does badly and which make him low in spirit, never thinks of washing pointless worries out of his mind, together with squalid little calculations and the dregs of low envy and greed that clog him and harm the sound functioning of his alimentary tract, heart and nervous system.

But cleaning out one's batteries is not enough; they also have to be recharged. Just as one's cares and worries foul up one's organs, so necessarily, there are states that favor their rejuvenation. A single word defines them all: happiness. . . .

Yes, your brain produces happiness! Your mind creates your Super Years. A Louis Harris poll, sponsored by the National Council on the Aging, indicates that older people generally have a more positive outlook on life than younger people do. Only 13 percent of the elderly respondents felt that loneliness was a significant problem, for example, as opposed to 65 percent of younger people.

Your brain is the rudder which steers your life's course. Marie Dressler wrote, in *My Own Story,* "One may be old or young at eighty. As for me, I have the blood of explorers in me and am out to conquer new worlds. I have no sense of having ended my career, but rather of having begun it. I'm starting out with a smile . . . I do not like a fight, but if one comes, I shall give it a hug and a kiss. I'm not afraid, for fear means death, and I know that the reaching out, giving out part of me, the part that likes to make people laugh and cry and be happy, can never die."

Out of *your* mind comes life, love, and energy. Guard it well—your precious mind!—the key that unlocks your life's overflowing treasure chest, the Super Years!

CHAPTER 3

Change Your Mind—and Live!

"WE don't die of old age," scientists state. "We die of *disease*." More and more researchers believe correct brain use actually slows the aging process. Conversely, they reason that incorrect brain input results in tremendously unsatisfactory feedback—unhealthy stress, illness, and premature aging.

You can change your mind—your negative mind-sets, that is—and live. Unquestionably you can live better; probably you'll also live longer.

Disease caused by stress produces illness and aging, researchers say. Stress changes our body cells, breaks down immune systems, causes cancers, heart disease, arthritis, and a host of lesser maladies.

But can it really be possible that the way we *program our brains* can work such havoc in our bodies and emotions? It's just that simple, according to scientists. Our wrong thinking inevitably leads to actions that hasten old age and shorten life. Unnecessary drugs, unrelieved tensions, unhealthy life-styles, emotional deprivation—those literally rob us of our best years.

Fortunately, there's an answer. Scientists assure us our minds can be retrained: new habits can be formed; the aging process can be dramatically reversed. Centuries ago, the apostle Paul advised the same thing: ". . . be ye transformed by the renewing of your mind. . ." (Romans 12:2).

Begin that transformation today. Make this year the first of many, many Super Years! Benjamin Franklin exemplified the power produced by an ever-renewed mind. He understood the force of *habit*. He set himself the task of changing one undesirable habit or character trait per year. Franklin kept daily written records. When his performance improved and the new habit became regular, he then concentrated on another area of change.

Franklin's diligence at *changing his mind* produced a life of prodigious work and ever-increasing genius. He still is considered the towering figure of his century, because he continually worked at changing and improving his mind.

Like Benjamin Franklin, you can identify the thinking that robs your life, then change those attitudes to life-giving ones!

It's exciting to decide: *It's time to change my life.*
It's fantastic to decide: *I can choose to be happy.*
It's important to decide: *I can be healthy, wealthy, and wise.*

William James, the noted pioneer American psychologist, advised, "Be not afraid of life. Believe that life is worth living, and your belief will help create the fact."

Life is worth living. Life is worth improving. Life is worth *extending*. Earl Nightingale, in one of his radio programs, listed fifteen ways to keep miserable.

1. Think about yourself.

2. Talk about yourself.

3. Use the personal pronoun *I* as often as possible.

4. Mirror yourself continually in the opinion of others.

5. Listen greedily to what people say about you.

6. Insist on consideration and respect.

7. Demand agreement with your own views on everything.

8. Sulk if people are not grateful to you for favors shown them.

9. Never forget a service you may have rendered.

10. Expect to be appreciated.

11. Be suspicious.

12. Be sensitive to slight.

13. Be jealous and envious.

14. Never forget a criticism.

15. Trust nobody but yourself.

What a list! Of course the author might have pointed out that those habits are aging, as well as misery making. "Old thinking" can exist in a young person, however, and "young thinking" in a very old person. The following story illustrates that point:

It seems that Dr. Albert Schweitzer, with his friend and biographer Erica Anderson, once offered a youthful hitchhiker a ride. The young man was on his way to join a religious order—from despair, rather than vocation. Dr. Schweitzer listened to his frustrations for a while, then spoke to his new friend from his heart. Erica Anderson wrote:

He stresses that one must never, out of despair, give up one's freedom. He talks to the young man, who does not believe in anything, of the obstacles and problems which life can bring, even in a religious order; of the futility of blind obedience without faith; of losing the respect of others in case one decides to leave an order and cannot any more.

He talks of the need to start anew when in despair, of the courage to try a fresh way of existence. For seven miles Dr. Schweitzer tries to touch something in the young man which still has a glimmer of faith, a spark of hope.

At last he (the passenger) speaks, with less bitterness and self-pity than before. "Maybe you have something," he said. "Maybe it is not a coincidence that you picked me up. I did not even bother to raise my hand for a lift any more. I was sure that people didn't care, that people are no good. I have no friend. . . ."

Here the good doctor interrupts him. "You must not expect anything—from others," Dr. Schweitzer says. "It's you yourself from whom you must ask a lot. Only from oneself has one the right to ask for everything or anything. This way it's up to yourself—your own choice. What you get from others remains a present, a gift."

At any age we can allow brain drain to begin. By midlife, however, many minds have begun to fill with negative notions. "I'm not getting any younger." "I plan to take it easy until I retire." "If I quit smoking, I'll gain weight." "I hate those young women, the way they dress, the way they flirt with my husband." "I can't do much about anything." "If I lose my job, start packing. We're going to the poorhouse." "You can't fight City Hall."

The place to fight City Hall begins within my Self. I'd better go straight to headquarters—my own mind. Someone up there needs straightening out. That someone is *me*. I can change my mind; my life depends upon that fact.

Check the following list of known killers. Each originates in your mind:

1. **Fear and Anxiety.** "He has not learned the lesson of life who does not every day surmount a fear," wrote Ralph Waldo Emerson. Fear, and that generalized, diffused cloud of fear we call "anxiety," becomes a way of life for many people. The phenomenal sale of tranquilizers and mood-elevating drugs amounts to a national disgrace in America. Fear, anxiety, and superfluous drugs can lead to intractable diseases.

As Lloyd Douglas said, "If a man harbors any sort of fear, it percolates through all his thinking, damages his personality, makes him landlord to a ghost."

You can learn to handle fear and anxiety. *You can change your mind.*

2. **Worry.** Poet Robert Frost said, "The reason why worry kills more people than work is that more people worry than work." Worry can produce several stress-caused diseases, as any physician knows. The worry habit (and it *is* a habit) needs to go. It's a killer. As Henry Ward Beecher said, "It is not work that kills men; it is worry. Worry is rust upon the blade."

By contrast, historian David S. Muzzey advised us to try *faith.* "Faith is courage," he wrote. "It is creative while despair is always destructive."

If you worry, *you can change your mind.*

3. **Pain and Grief.** It's evident that every life will contain some dark days, desperate grief, or dreary discontent. Instead of programming yourself for dread, however, you can prepare to withstand the tough times. The apostle Paul wrote in Romans 8:37, "In all these things [trials] we are more than conquerors. . . ."

"Joy comes, grief goes, we know not how," observed James Russell Lowell. When you encounter deep grief or severe pain, you can learn to look for redemptive factors within your experiences. As Horace Greeley said, "Great grief makes sacred those upon whom its hand is laid. Joy may elevate, ambition glorify, but only sorrow can consecrate."

Physical, mental, or emotional pain, grief and sorrow, illness and suffering, can refine and ennoble your life. You can prepare your mind to receive tough challenges with courage. If you have chosen the way of bitterness instead, *you can change your mind.*

4. **Anger and Resentment.** Not only the length of your life, but the *quality*, will be attacked by these twin devastators. Any list of major diseases, including cancer, arthritis, as well as suicide and mental illness, relates to the twin demons of anger and resentment.

Our bodies can't put up with sustained doses of such emotional poison. "Anger blows out the lamp of the mind," someone once stated. However, the reverse also is true. The lamp of your mind can illuminate those dark corners where ill feeling dwells. Even if anger has become your life-style, *you can change your mind.*

5. **Depression.** Someone has called depression the most common disease in our nation. Defined as "anger turned inward," depression left untreated can result in a catalog of physical and emotional ills.

One grandmother, angry and depressed because she was aging and didn't like it, sought medical help. "Limit your depression," her doctor advised. "Permit yourself no more than fifteen minutes a day. The antidote to depression is activity. When your fifteen minutes is up, work at something!"

After a lifelong habit of depression, the woman learned *she could change her mind.*

6. **Unforgiveness.** Inability to forgive can make you sick. As Henry Ward Beecher said, " 'I can forgive, but I cannot forget,'

is only another way of saying, 'I cannot forgive.' "

Nearly two thousand years ago, a Man came into this world and taught a radical concept called *forgiveness* to a people used to obtaining "an eye for an eye, a tooth for a tooth."

"Forgiveness is a lifesaver," one psychiatrist stated. "If God hadn't taught us how to forgive, psychiatry would have had to invent it. There is no other way, sometimes, to wipe the emotional slate clean and get on with a healthy life."

The individual who refuses to forgive unwittingly hugs a sharp knife to himself. "Let me be a little kinder, let me be a little blinder, to the faults of those around me . . ." Edgar Guest wrote. If you find forgiveness hard to do, you can learn how. *You can change your mind.*

7. **Boredom.** Yes, boredom can shorten your life. It leads to inertia, lack of physical and mental activity, failure of the imagination, and disinterest in vital action and choices.

Boredom, left to itself, produces immeasurable stress. It discolors your world. "Do not expect the world to look bright, if you habitually wear gray-brown glasses," advised Charles W. Eliot.

It's easy enough to get your glasses changed. *You can change your mind.*

Life events, as well as daily attitudes, can produce negative mind-sets like those just listed, of course. When devastating events send your life into a spin, the answer is *action,* according to Dr. Paul L. Walker, noted Atlanta minister, psychologist and author. "Whether it's job loss, marital breakup, financial crisis or what, get going immediately," Dr. Walker stresses. "Don't flounder, and don't wait for things to right themselves.

"Go for counseling. With a trained, competent counselor, do these four things:

1. Explore your feelings.

2. Look at possibilities.

3. Help develop a plan of action.

4. Follow up with periodic reinforcement."

Dr. Walker believes we should focus on *behavior* when crisis strikes. "Many people become immobilized. They begin to enjoy their own pity party," he commented. "Remember, it's important not to waste time. Decide on a plan and begin to work it out. You can do it!"

When you put your brain in gear, the whole machine moves forward. Life can assume its normal momentum. Once again, your brain puts *you* at the wheel—shifting gears as you need to, coasting only if you wish. The healthy, well-used brain can find the best roads, even the shortcuts. It can steer you straight into your Super Years, despite the worst sort of roadblocks and obstacles.

Even the very aged can handle disaster well, Dr. Walker believes. Despite physical infirmities, loneliness, or other deprivation, he insists our latter years can contain tremendous victory and fulfillment. Dr. Walker suggests these steps toward confident living:

1. Accept yourself, with your limitations.

2. Change your toys. Choose a new set of diversions. Fill up your mind more.

3. Use your body. It's made to be used. It's a matter of keeping it in tune.

4. Learn your limits. Then learn where you're unlimited.

These decisions will require inner direction. The positive-thinking brain can and will make decisions. You can do it now, before crisis comes. You can decide to operate from the strengths in your life, rather than the weaknesses. Thus you train your brain to love, laugh, enjoy, and create. You reinforce your powers to withstand life's assaults. Above all, you enrich your life daily.

You can change your mind. You can decide today to encourage everything about your life toward health, vigor, and blessing. You can abolish anger, fear, unforgiveness, depression, and negative thinking of every sort.

By all means get professional counseling if you need it. As Dr. Walker advises, "Don't just stand there, do something!" Develop an action plan. The alternative—inaction and passivity—literally will rob you of precious life.

Dr. Albert Schweitzer's noble phrase "reverence for life" belongs to all of us. We respond to the truth of those words. Something in us yearns toward life—abundant life. The contemplation of life, with its depths, its mysteries and its miracles, makes all souls bow in reverence and awe.

Therefore choose life. Your brain contains a secret weapon which protects you from negative thinking and safeguards your precious inner Self. That guardian? *Desire!*

That powerful, driving force—*desire*—will guide you into your Super Years. You can cultivate that gift. Even if you've nearly forgotten how, you can learn to desire again.

You *can* change your mind. You *can* utilize desire!

CHAPTER 4

Your Heart's Desires

Your desires. Tap into those, and you discover much about your Self. Trust your deep desires, and you learn to trust that Self. Encounter the force behind the truest truths within you, and you're in touch with your Creator. In that way, at least, we mirror Him.

How simple! Your desires actually reveal your Self to yourself, and to the world. How simple—and yet, how few of us make the effort.

How well do you know your Self? That's easy enough to discover. Ask this one question, for starters: What is the one big, all-important thing for which you want your entire life to stand?

Perhaps you can answer that one immediately. Or perhaps you'll begin to think. As you get more and more in touch with yourself, you'll discover a world of new energy beginning to bubble. New desires will begin to emerge. Astonishing ideas will pop up. You'll imagine more to cram into your Super Years than you ever dreamed might exist for you!

At this point, let's clarify the word *desire*. Webster defines it this way: *to wish or long for; want; crave. Something or someone longed for.* We might ask ourselves, how long has it been since we really craved, really experienced a longing? For that matter, how long since we've felt real, honest-to-goodness hunger? We commonly learn to muffle desires and satiate hungers before they begin to surface. We blunt the edges and smooth the surfaces of our own instincts, then wonder why we can't hear our inner voice when it tries to speak to us from the heart.

Begin to desire desire. Long for it. Seek it. With fresh desire, you'll find a rush of new life. Your Super Years need the strength and pure focus of your very specific desires. These can literally propel you into change, growth, risk, and nobility of purpose. You have everything to gain!

At 60, Mattie Lou O'Kelley, one of America's most famous contemporary folk artists, began to paint her own enchanting impressions of hilly North Georgia landscapes. She'd scarcely ever held a brush. She believed you had to attend art school in order to paint. She read art books, but didn't understand the instructions.

Nevertheless, Mattie Lou O'Kelley followed her instincts. She mixed colors her own way, painted what she saw in her own mind's eye. Today, at 74, her paintings hang in the American Museum of Folk Art. Her work is sought out by such notables as former President Jimmy Carter, and a lifetime ambition has been realized with the publication of *A Winter Place,* a collection of paintings which illustrate a poem by Ruth Yaffe Radin. Presently she's at work on a pictorial autobiography of her childhood and life on a Georgia farm.

Your heart's desire! That's the "you" nobody else can discover. That's the unique personage that enriches the rest of us. You'll never outgrow your need to express, fulfill, and enjoy that desire. Once out of touch, however, how in the world can you locate the desires that can begin once again to light up your life?

Artist-designer Gloria Vanderbilt outlines a fascinating method. In her book *Woman to Woman,* Gloria Vanderbilt offers a tremendously revealing way to discover things you'd forgotten about yourself—or perhaps never knew. Here's how to take some personal inner measurements. On a large sheet of paper, write:

MY PERSONAL INVENTORY

1. Beside the left margin of the paper, write as many numbers as the years of your life, one number beneath the other. Turn the page if you run out of space.

2. Think of things that give you pleasure. Jot down quick words or phrases, in no particular order, one beside each number. Fill out the list. If you are 62, you should list 62 "pleasures."

3. Put a check mark beside each activity listed that you enjoy doing on your own; a plus mark if you prefer doing it with others; two plus marks if there is a special person with whom you like to share it. For example: "Walking in the rain with Joe" rates two pluses.

4. Place a dollar sign after items that cost money.

5. Circle numbers beside items that would not have been on your list five years ago. Underline items you want on your list ten years from now. (If you use different colored pens for these various exercises, you easily begin to see a pattern emerge.)

This astonishing exploration—(fun for the family to try, great fun for a party)—reveals quite a bit. Had you forgotten how much you love to sing? Did you know you hope always to live somewhere near the ocean? Did you imagine animals—especially pets—need to come back into your life?

Also, take a look at your pluses. Study these carefully, and you begin to get insight into your needs for more alone time or more sociability.

Don't take this inventory too seriously, however. It's not a test, but simply a means of self-discovery. One group decided their pleasures weren't serious enough. "Everything on page one shows I'm materialistic!" protested a shocked young woman. "Clothes, fur coat, new automobile, diamonds. . . ."

"It could show you enjoy beauty, fashion, and a successful lifestyle," an older woman objected. "What's so bad about that? You're enjoying beautiful things, not worshiping them."

"Almost everything I thought about involved food," a grandfather observed drily. "Did anybody else's list start with hot cornbread?"

Despite the jokes, insights came. A gray-haired woman shyly admitted she'd listed "hugs." Nearly everyone included babies, flowers, love songs.

Pleasures or needs? Where do you draw the line? That's a serious question. The life large enough to include great joy invariably spills over and blesses us all. The psalmist wrote, "Delight yourself in the Lord, and he will give you the desires of your heart" (*see* Psalms 37:4). To be delighted with the Author of all life is really to experience life—and to know the One who placed desire within you, even as you were created.

Cherish the desires so peculiarly your own. Nurture them and allow them to flower. These will empower and color the rest of your days, and thereby enhance us all.

Here is another way to contact your present desires. On a large sheet of paper, write:

I WANT

1. *Quickly list as many desires as come to mind.* Write in no particular order of importance. List something small (chocolate

ripple ice cream) as readily as something enormous (world peace). When your imagination slows, quit writing. You can add other items later.

2. *Place a check mark beside anything you can give yourself today:* (a movie; a bubble bath; that new book you've wanted; a jaunt to the nursery for a flat of marigolds).

3. *Take a good look at the remaining items.* What nuggets do you discover? Don't dismiss them too rapidly. You'd like to learn to ski. You wish you could visit your married daughter. You'd love to rearrange your workshop.

4. *Dig deep into your thinking.* Maybe you'd like to commit time, money, or even just a decision. You *will* work for your political party. You *can* take those night courses at your community college. It *is* time to take a month off and write; teach your granddaughters to embroider; learn how to square dance; give a surprise party for the friend who nursed you through pneumonia, bought your groceries, and heard your complaints.

Does all this sound too simple? It is simple, yet not easy. Sometimes it's hard to make a decision; hard to jolt oneself out of a rut; hard even to do a small thing without first consulting others.

Your Super Years should contain a wealth of small delights. Then comes the paradox, of course—that of realizing how often *small* equals *perfect*. The one first pink rose . . . the bowl of hot, butter-fragrant popcorn with a certain small boy . . . the fresh coconut cake you happened to bake the day someone came dragging home, worn out and peevish . . . the glorious day you balance the checkbook!

Get in touch with your *I wants.* Learn more about yourself in the process. Are they large? Small? Selfish? Imaginative? Profitable to you or others? Exciting? Possible?

Worry not. Mature desires won't make you selfish. They'll just put joy in your heart, a spring in your step, and excitement in your life. So will you set a good pace for others to follow—the dear, good others in your family; the wonderful others in your personal world.

Desire empowers your life. Thank God for your own unique outlook. It can lead straight into discovery of the new life you're ready to lead.

Begin to desire. It's your catalyst into the Super Years!

CHAPTER 5

Super Job Success

THE newspaper headline read, AT 70, HIS BEST WORK MAY BE AHEAD. The story concerned a symphony orchestra conductor, but it could just as well be you.

Vocationally, you could be headed for some of the richest pastures imaginable, if you wish. There's far less talk these days about "older workers" and "retirees," but some real horn blowing concerning "mature talent" and "proven skills." American thinking is changing where you and your work future is concerned. If you enjoy working, want to continue work, or would like to embark on new work, your timing could hardly be better.

Decades ago, publisher E. W. Bok stated: "At age fifty a man's real life begins. He has acquired upon which to achieve; received from which to give; learned from which to teach; cleared from which to build."

You can decide to build as big as you desire. Your "real life," your Super Years, could explode with success. Stories about mid-life and later-life career exploits no longer boggle our minds; they have become quite commonplace. With pension funds, the U.S. Social Security system, and mandatory retirement age in question, it makes super sense to survey with a keen eye your skills, job assets, and attitudes toward working.

First, though, consider the word *success*. What does that word mean to you, as related to your career or work future? Perhaps you never thought much about success, or you unconsciously believed your chances dwindled once Middle Age set in. Not so. At any age you can be productively, gainfully, and joyfully employed. As Helen Gurley Brown, author and editor, attested, ". . . the most successful I've been is in my fifties, when everything that was *going* to take hold has had a chance to *take* hold!

"Once in a while you have a setback—lost job, company politics you couldn't get out of the way of, horrendous personal problems—men, love, health, money—but as you get older, you get stronger. . . ."

Colonel Harlan Sanders knew that. He was well into his sixties when he launched his famous fried-chicken empire. He became hugely successful, widely copied, and a wealthy man.

Loretta Corcoran at 92 probably is America's oldest fashion model, earning 75 dollars per hour, according to *Family Circle* magazine. Working some twenty-five modeling jobs per year, Loretta says, "I find it's fun. I don't know why all the young models complain."

The same article reported there's a doctor who still makes house calls—at age 81! Dr. Paul Marston of Kezar Falls, Maine, even in the worst New England weather ventures out at night when patients get sick.

Then there's Ruth Hutchinson, 88, who reportedly is America's oldest disc jockey. She has a one-hour show every Wednesday night on radio station KSHE in Saint Louis, Missouri, and is popular with the rock 'n' roll set. "She's our superstar," her station manager says.

Or take conductor Leopold Stokowski, who renewed his recording contract for another five years—when he was 95!

You, too, probably can work as long as you want to work. The question is, what are your plans? What do you desire?

Some people, like my mother, decide to cut back their work hours. At 80 Mother gave up her normal 40- to 60-hour work week as a law clerk, electing to work on a consulting basis instead. "Part time is okay. I feel like just fooling around for a while," she explained. "Besides, I have all those people who want me to do their income tax returns. . . ."

Then, there was Arthur Fiedler, who for more than fifty years conducted the famous Boston Pops Orchestra—the longest career span for any conductor in all musical history. If anything, Fiedler believed in expanding his work life year by year, so that his most magnificent accomplishments took place toward the end of that unparalleled career. At 77, he created a motto: HE WHO RESTS, ROTS. He plastered those words all over Symphony Hall. "That's become my slogan, the words I live by," he stated.

Harry Ellis Dickson, Fiedler's associate conductor, long-time colleague and biographer, describes that supercharged life-style: "Characteristic of the perpetual motion that for so many years marked his career were four months in 1972, beginning in January and ending with the opening of the Boston Pops season at the end of April.

"Arthur was then seventy-seven years of age. He toured Japan, returned to the United States to take the Boston Pops Touring Orchestra on a thirteen-thousand-mile tour—including its first appearance at Carnegie Hall—after that, he gave two concerts with the Memphis Symphony and conducted eight more performances in a twelve-day period with the Syracuse Symphony. . . ."

Just past his eightieth birthday, Fiedler told an interviewer,

". . . I'm still going strong. Perhaps much too much so. But I like my work, and I think activity is the best thing in the world for you. If you're not active, you deteriorate. You might as well give up. People ask me, 'When are you going to retire?' I'm not even thinking about retirement. . . ."

If you truly desire challenging, rewarding work, you can find it at any age. Many people do not believe that. They point to today's high unemployment figures, point also to the thousands of young and able-bodied workers presently without jobs. The implication is, if young, healthy, skilled workers can't find employment, who will hire someone even older?

Actually, job attainment and success have very little to do with age. Desire, perseverance, imagination, flexibility, character, and know-how mean far more than one's birth date. Many of us allow ourselves to be brainwashed by employment agency personnel to believe we're pretty well washed up vocationally once we're past fifty. "In that case, change agencies," one executive advised. "Find one that specializes in placing mature workers. Refuse to buy the myth that you are unemployable."

You need to dispel those myths for yourself. Unless you are convinced you're well worth employing, you'll almost certainly send signals that you feel too old to be considered a fully worthwhile worker. For example, how do you react to some of these "myths"?

If a man doesn't make it by forty, he'll never make it. Nonsense! Men past forty take something called "early retirement" these days, then plunge into second or even third careers. They unload responsibilities that no longer thrill them, then find new horizons. Often they achieve financial success beyond their wildest dreams.

At 65, 80, or any other age, a man can become an "overnight success."

I'm just a housewife. So many of us answer to that description—and then we change. "Just a housewife" writes a best-seller; franchises the little idea she worked up in her spare time; markets her bread, pie, or fudge nationally; trains housemaids; earns fur coats and automobiles by distributing cosmetics, household supplies, vitamin products, home accessories, skin-care items, or anything else at all.

The little guy can't get anywhere these days. Look again! Even with very little capital, ingenious and industrious Americans somehow manage to accomplish astonishing success. An aircraft engineer retired, then borrowed money from relatives and friends to manufacture a product his colleagues predicted would fail. Today he and his two partners are millionaires.

No training. Everything is so specialized these days, so I'm just out in the cold. By Middle Age, every one of us has *some* training. Ordinary skills you take completely for granted—such things as child care, carpentry, gardening, or cooking—can lead you into tremendously improved financial health.

It takes thought, imagination, and action—but you already have enough skills to make a good living. Use what you have!

There's nothing for old people to do. I'm housebound, you know. That myth gets disproved every day! A wheelchair occupant keeps herself nicely by sewing hems for pay. Secretaries in a nearby office tower are delighted to bring dresses to her for one-day alterations. She has all the business she can handle!

An octogenarian man in a remote mountain village mails

gourd seeds and information to growers all over the world. Fascinated by gourds, he has become an authority on the subject. Though he hardly ever travels outside his steep village, except to the post office, he manages to make his hobby pay off handsomely: additional income; physical benefits from the gardening and other work; mental benefits from experimenting, corresponding, and dealing with new friends from many countries in the world; and even the additional hobby of stamp collecting, an offshoot of his letters from gourd growers on every continent.

You can no doubt think of many such entrepreneurs among your older friends. A house builder, bedfast after his second heart attack, amused himself by drawing patterns for wooden toys he could build while recuperating. His Early-American-style rocking horses, wagons, and other toys charmed boutique owners and collectors. He had to expand his toy line and bring his son into the business. "We're having a ball!" he exclaimed. Like many another older person who encounters a surprising new business success, the builder discovered the truth within an old slogan: WHEN LIFE HANDS YOU A LEMON, MAKE LEMONADE!

Perhaps you're ready to expand your own job or career horizons. Where do you look? First, look within yourself. Probe your mind. Try to discover some of the most exciting things you could do, then mentally try them on for size.

Let your mind go. Don't think too much about *reality* (make that *doubts*) at first, but simply let your ideas flow. Begin to list everything you do well, plus everything you'd enjoy trying or experiencing during your lifetime. Don't stop to evaluate, but simply *list*. If you're 92, and always wanted to be a fashion model, remember Loretta Corcoran! Assume that anything is possible. It just might be!

Write every desire or idea that comes to mind; then take a good look at what you've got. Magic tricks? Pony rides for children? Baking wedding cakes or sending care packages to students? Teaching Spanish? Selling boat plans? Quilt patterns? These and other equally simple skills proved to be highly marketable and enormously enjoyable for those who decided to turn them into a business.

Some of my desires (my lifelong dream of making a parachute jump, for example) look totally out of the question. Others, (working as a waitress or a travel guide), still could be attained.

Place a check beside everything on your list for which you have experience or know-how, or both. You *know* you can market those. Now look at those still untried desires. Number them according to preference. How many of those ideas could be turned into your next job?

For example, a woman who always loved dolls now turns out expensive, custom-designed doll babies on a well-paid business basis. A man who loves to travel found a way to fly first class to his job at parades and football games throughout the United States—selling balloons. He works hard, earns a high five-figure income, enjoys his life of adventure and change—and there's no one to tell him he's too old to do it!

These are two examples of ingenious people who made their interests and desires pay off for them. You can think of many others. You also—with that same sort of imagination—can find a job idea equally fulfilling and profitable for *you*. Think. Then allow yourself to daydream and desire. J. Paul Getty offered the formula for financial and job success: "Find a need and fill it." At any time of life, that formula applies.

A canvass of preretirement and postretirement workers turned up some interesting advice about job hunting and career changes.

Some companies, like IBM, offer tuition to employees and their spouses approaching retirement. They can study real estate, small-business management, and other subjects to help them start a second career or ease into retirement. Your company might have an education program available.

Read the Want Ads. "Don't assume you're too old for the job you want," dark-eyed Ellen advised. "I was forty-six and had no work experience. I didn't even know what to wear to a job interview, or what to say when I got there.

"I simply liked the job description, so I went after it. I felt so scared, I wore my fur coat and best shoes, then walked tall to keep my knees from knocking." To her amazement, Ellen got the job. Within a year she was promoted to division sales manager, one of the five territories within a national company. "I ignored the subject of age," she said. "I'm so glad I did. It just never came up!"

With the list of things you enjoy doing, head for your nearest public library. Ask your librarian for a directory of local business firms; then spend a few hours checking out the sort of jobs which might match up with your skills. "That sort of research always gets results," a professional headhunter said. "The person who knows what he likes to do and goes after it almost always succeeds in finding work. Employers are impressed by that kind of initiative."

Place an ad in your local newspaper, or post notices on church, shopping-center or office bulletin boards. "My neighborhood ads brought me more extra typing jobs than I could handle," a retired secretary told me. She now runs a typing service, staffed by three other women who work part-time, with her spare bedroom serving as an office. "I never dreamed it would grow this big, but I love it," she said. "I enjoy running my own business. Also, I found I *needed* the stimulus, and the new faces in my life."

Consider sales work. Even if you've never sold anything before, you might discover innate sales ability you never dreamed you had—and it could make you wealthy. A beautician who could neither read nor write began to sell cosmetics. When her sales volume soared, she found herself confronted with an enormous personal challenge—the need to surmount illiteracy. Her colleagues encouraged her to put aside long-standing feelings of inadequacy and shame, and helped her learn to read manuals and write sales orders.

Despite a handicap far beyond anything most of us face, the beautician overcame her illiteracy, earned thousands of extra dollars and company prizes, learned to drive a car, and got a driver's license—all in one year!

Men and women from every profession, and from all walks of life, find personal sales offer challenge and growth potential beyond anything they've ever known. You might explore the idea with *successful* friends in direct-selling organizations. Ask them about drawbacks and pitfalls, as well as the obvious potential in such work. If they're making it, they know what works. They can give you realistic advice and answers.

Look for an employment service that specializes in placing older workers. Many cities have such agencies. If yours does not, consider approaching a church, YMCA, or civic organization about establishing such a service. Be persistent. Seek, and you will find.

Think ahead to logical offshoots from your present career. A network television program featured a 90-year-old former ballet dancer who teaches dancing to anyone—old or young—for one dollar a lesson. Skinny little girls, dumpy housewives, grand-mothers—all who ever dreamed of dancing—there they were, working at the *barre,* under the eagle-eyed tutelage of a grande dame who still has a passion for ballet and knows how to share it.

Think of similar variations on your personal theme. An attorney who retires to seacoast life in California might specialize in maritime law, for example. Or a college professor expert in languages might support herself by translating business letters and documents for companies with branches or customers in other countries. An airline pilot might open his own travel agency. And so on.

Remember to tell people that you desire new work. Let them know. Your pastor, co-workers, neighbors, brother-in-law, *anyone* might help you make that vital connection. "Word of mouth is very valuable," one woman said. "Don't underestimate it."

Mainly, though, it's important to raise your own consciousness regarding job possibilities. They'll exist for you all your life. Begin now to look around, research, consider, *think.* You'll discover so many potential sources for unlocking your money-making talents and heading yourself towards greater job success. The public library. Placement services at church, civic club, or community centers. Networking. Word of mouth. Advertisements.

You can enjoy the fulfillment of meaningful work as long as you live, if you:

1. Resolve to do so.

2. Desire and expect to stay occupied with interesting and rewarding plans.

3. Take time to know yourself better than you ever did in the past.

4. Find out what you want to do, then go for it.

5. Don't listen to anyone who says you can't.

6. Aim high, and continue to set your sights *higher*.

7. Believe in yourself.

8. Continue to think, dream, desire, and plan.

9. Remember the words of Sir Winston Churchill, himself an old man at the time, who advised: "Never give in, never give in, never, never, *never* ... !"

CHAPTER 6

Your Money, More or Less

BY now—facing your Super Years—you're dedicated not just to making a living, but making a *life*. How much money do you want? How much do you need? How much money is *too* much money—is there any such thing?

Until you can answer those questions for yourself with true self-knowledge, your Super Years remain up for grabs. Amazingly enough, however, most of us *don't* know the answers. Attitudes toward money appear almost as personal and individualistic as fingerprints—and we don't know our fingerprints, either.

Skip this chapter, if you're well acquainted with your own fiscal attitudes, ideas, and goals. But if, like the majority of us, you too often stumble through today's monetary maze, hoping to grope your way into a clearing—read on. The shape of your future largely depends upon your willingness to:

Take charge of your finances. Recognize that you must begin the vital task of understanding where you are and where you're going. Like everyone else, you need a financial plan.

Learn how to manage your holdings. No matter how vast or how tiny it may be, your estate is your responsibility. Even if you enlist a professional money manager to handle it, you should understand what he or she is attempting to do for you.

Decide to make money management a serious segment of your life. With even a small amount of study, reading, or consulting with bank, insurance, or tax experts, you might produce some handsome dividends.

Set aside some time each week for this purpose. If you faithfully budget even one or two hours per week for bill paying, record keeping, or financial study, you'll find new ways to:

Increase what you have.

Cut expenses.

Learn how to get what you want for little or no monetary exchange.

In this chapter, you're challenged to think of ways you can significantly expand your options. Know this: *Your Super Years can yield steadily increasing personal prosperity. Even at your present income level, you can learn to live richer by living smarter.*

How much richer? You might be amazed at what you can do for yourself if you try. I believe Benjamin Franklin would urge you to take hold of your monetary perspective and examine it hard. Franklin respected thrift and shrewd money usage, and warned, "Poverty often deprives a man of all spirit and virtue; an empty bag cannot stand upright."

Ralph Waldo Emerson offered an even more succinct observation on the subject: "Money represents the price of life." Since you choose life, you owe yourself the benefits of deciding *this minute* to learn better how to use, enjoy, conserve, guard, increase, and share your wealth. And it *is* a decision. The moment we decide to spring ourselves from a monetary trap, we're on our way.

The key word? Action! As Henry Ford said, "Money is like an arm or leg—use it or lose it." Ask yourself, *Do I know how to use money, or do I simply spend it?* Again, action becomes the byword. Its opposite, *passivity,* produces some common and dismaying symptoms: monetary paralysis; fiscal ignorance; something-for-nothing grabbiness; financial fatalism; and a dreary poverty syndrome born of fear and apprehension.

Fortunately, it's never too late to learn even the most basic facts of life. And money facts *are* basic. They underlie every attitude and decision you project. Money, or lack of it, colors your life. Sometimes it actually can rule your life. Even a surplus of the lovely stuff can divert the unwary into some decidedly unlovely channels, on occasion. As Emerson sagely observed, "Money often costs too much."

When Two Are Better Than One. Money discussions help you and your spouse view your world and your future. How do you feel about money as relating to self-worth, security, pleasure, leisure, extravagance, and other hard-to-measure values? When one or the other is "funny" about money, or even dreads discussing the subject, there's a diplomatic answer—perhaps attending a college short course or a community seminar concerning money, for starters.

Or choose an area of mutual interest (a trip to Europe, helping to educate a talented grandchild, or updating the family home) and brainstorm together, looking for creative ways to finance your project.

Try to *involve* that passive partner. Encourage. Get excited about the possibilities for attaining your joint desires and projects. Determine to *honestly* explore your feelings about such things as giving, receiving, helping, planning, earning, saving, and any other loaded subject you both learned to avoid in the past.

"Ed and I never saw eye-to-eye about money. He's ultraconservative, always looking over his shoulder for something. I was always telling him, 'You make a good living, we have everything we need; why do you worry all the time?' " Anne confided.

"When we joined an investment club, I told Ed it would just make us fight. I'm real easygoing about finances, but he's not. Instead, I learned that for thirty-two years my husband has felt he might make a big mistake that would cost us everything. He might lose his job, we might lose our home, and so on. 'That's *crazy*,' I told him. 'All these years you've taken care of me and our two boys much better than average. What could make you afraid?' "

Anne flashed a quick, sympathetic smile, then glanced at the diamond rings on her beautifully manicured hands. "Men," she said with a little laugh. "I've learned more about Ed since joining his silly investment club than anything else we've done together. I learned how much he dislikes risk. Also, that he doesn't know how to tell me when things bother him. Of course, he never really knew how to show his feelings very well—but I didn't know he *had* feelings about money.

"I'm trying to learn," she told me. "I want to understand my husband, and what makes him tick. The more I learn about finance, the more I realize how smart Ed really is. I tell him so, too!"

Ed and Anne are learning to communicate about money. They're beginning to understand themselves better, and feel good about reenforcing one another in this important area of life. Ask yourself: Do I communicate well with my mate about money?

Could we—and should we—improve? How could we go about establishing a more comfortable basis for "money talk"?

Trade Your Soft Intentions for Hard Cash. Do you feel overwhelmed by the challenge of trying to organize your untidy financial affairs? You're not alone. Many another man or woman faces another twenty, thirty, or even fifty years of further fiscal chaos—unless someone helps him or her turn over a new leaf.

Fortunately, there's a world of help out there for those of us who need it. First, however, *I must face the fact that I need help.* Second, *I must seek it.* I need to resolve to untangle those snarled affairs, to find the end of the string and begin to work on the knot.

Where to begin? First, *visualize*—really imagine—the joy you'll feel when you've solved your problem(s). Imagine yourself taking it, a step at a time, until you've tidied up every aspect of your financial life. Give yourself a deadline—three months, six months, two years—to learn and put into practice the things you need to do.

Next, you might head for the library. Check out two or three basic books on personal finance. Devote yourself to a weekend or so of serious reading (possibly some of the most profitable reading you'll accomplish this year). Begin to list items that need further study: insurance, perhaps, record keeping, or investment strategies.

From there you can take it any number of ways. You'll find a wealth of free, published material offered by banks, insurance companies, and securities firms, for example. Also, your attorney, financial planner, insurance agent, stockbroker, accountant or banker can recommend courses, seminars, or specific reading materials to zero in on your particular needs.

The decision to do some detective work starts a process. From there, follow your nose. Ask questions. Read. Be available for research. "And don't feel intimidated," my friend Irene advised. "Nobody comes into this world knowing how to balance a checkbook. So get started. It really doesn't matter where, just start!

"My husband walked away after twenty-three years of marriage, leaving me with no idea of how to budget, pay bills, or anything else. What's more, I had inherited a terrible credit rating. At first I wanted to kill myself.

"It took a year, but I learned. By the time I got the bills paid off and had some idea of where I was going, I enrolled in a college evening course in investing. Meanwhile I had rented, then arranged to buy, my own first investment—a duplex.

"One evening I asked my professor for some advice. He said he had none! If I'd managed to pull out of debt, buy my first property, and live debt-free and rent-free, he said I should be teaching his class. Not bad for a lady past fifty, scared to death, and totally ignorant about money!"

Like Irene, you can find all the help you need. Simply decide now to *trade your years of soft intentions for good hard cash*. What a trade—cash instead of chaos. Just think, you can stop procrastinating and begin to untangle even a seemingly hopeless monetary snarl. You can begin *today* to finance your Super Years!

How to Spend Less and Have More. There's a real art to acquiring the things that really matter to you in this life—especially when you live within a fixed income. As Henry David Thoreau wrote, "Money is not required to buy one necessity of the soul."

More and more, you can learn how to spend less and less and still live like royalty. How? Through study. Simply survey every aspect of your life as you live it, or wish to live it. Then devote some time, thought, and effort to finding ways to upgrade your living for little or nothing.

What do you want and need? Better health? Better looks? A more desirable environment? Travel? College courses? Mental stimulus? Music, art, the humanities? These things can be costly, yet all can be obtained for little or no cash exchange, if you know how to do it.

Call it "creative financing." Call it barter, a swap meet, resourcefulness, American ingenuity. At the risk of sounding simplistic, there really are (as the old Irish proverb says) more ways to kill a cat than choking it to death with cream.

Larry knows that. He loves to travel, but can't afford the tariff. He "sold himself" to a bus line as a tour guide to scenic New England. From there on, it was a cinch. After several satisfying trips throughout the USA, he progressed to cruise ships, university-sponsored art tours, to guiding groups through Israel. "It's the best of all possible worlds," Larry says. "Strenuous, sure. Not everybody's cup of tea. Working with a travel agency, though, I put together tours of Spain, Greece, Germany, all my dream countries. I'm learning a lot and lovin' it!"

Long before "networking" became a buzzword, Hazel Mebane exploited the idea. Tiny, fragile-appearing Hazel hardly looks like someone who'd be capable of household restoration and heavy cleaning. Still, that's exactly what she does—with a little help from her friends.

Gifted with exceptional imagination, good German thoroughness and elbow grease, Hazel will tackle the world's dingiest house and polish through decades of grime to basic, shining cleanliness. She keeps elaborate files on hundreds of housekeeping aids. When she lacks answers, Hazel phones the factory and gets 'em.

"America is filled with 'throwaway' houses," she told me.

"People let them run down, then they move. A house that's not maintained produces dispirited occupants. People's minds get as cluttered and filmed-over as their dwellings do."

Hazel offers answers to the sick, discouraged or poverty-ridden. "Upgrade! You'll have to let go of your pride and allow your friends and family to help you. You learn to swap labor, tools, ideas, expertise, and strength. With my methods, anyone can upgrade their house one hundred percent at very little monetary cost."

Hazel, who presently is compiling a book of her methods and philosophies, maintains that any householder who fails to "network" is throwing away money by the bushel. She believes men and women should form housework teams to do heavy cleaning, decorating projects or restoration work, working in groups of two or four on a regular schedule. "My friend Gloria and I have cleaned one another's houses for years," she said. "We know everything about each other. Any false pride or sensitivity I might feel about anyone looking behind my range or in my closets went out the window years ago.

"Team cleaning is the way to train our kids. We teach; they supply the muscles. It's the way to give ourselves to the ill, the elderly, or people with temporary problems. It's the way to keep our houses in good repair, spend little money, and increase our investments. Also, it's all-American!"

That same efficiency translates into many other areas of swapping and bartering. More than three hundred barter clubs across America accept members who wish to swap goods or services. (The IRS considers all trades as taxable income, of course, so keep scrupulous records.) By means of computers, "buyers" and "sellers" are matched, records kept, and a wondrous variety of options opened to those with more gumption than money.

Your community may have a barter club, as do many large and small church denominations. An artist swaps paintings for his family's dental work; a mother prepares tax returns in exchange for having her daughter's wedding reception catered and her wedding gown custom-made; a widower exchanges small repair jobs for a supply of homemade casseroles and "real" bread. An elderly woman swaps a bedroom and kitchen privileges to a medical student, who watches her furnace, cuts her grass and shops for her groceries. And so it goes.

You have something to trade. Make a list of the three things you most need or desire right now, then brainstorm. If you hired Laura to redesign your living room, how could you pay her without using money? What could you swap for health spa privileges? How could you "finance" a vacation, a pickup truck, a college degree, with no money? (Or very little money.)

More and more Americans are discovering answers to these questions. Here are suggestions to start you thinking:

• *Some 500 colleges across America offer a summer vacation week of study and change of scene for a modest tuition.* Ask your local college, library, or write to Elderhostel, 100 Boylston St., Suite 200, Boston, Massachusetts 02116.

• *Ask about senior citizen discounts before patronizing theaters, bus/rail/airlines, restaurants, and stores.* More and more merchants offer discounts these days. Have a driver's license, Medicare card, or some other proof of age to offer.

• *Use, use, use your public library.* You'll find everything from the latest thriller to the finest art reproductions available on loan. New books, old recipes, paintings, sculptures, classical records or jazz, foreign language cassettes, video movies, sometimes even potted plants, are yours—free for the asking. Your library also sponsors free seminars and lectures on public affairs, cultural themes, and current studies. It's a bargain!

• *Look for ways to cut medical costs.* A recent article in *Money* magazine advocates negotiating fees with your doctor or dentist, if you feel entitled to a discount. Learn about generic and mail-order drugs which can save you money. Or join the American Association of Retired Persons (AARP, 215 Long Beach Blvd., Long Beach, California 90801). Buy drugs by mail through that organization for substantial discounts. You might consider having routine dentistry done by dental students if you live near a dental school, or seek out a clinic run by a hospital.

• *Find ways to dress better for less.* Six women brought their clothing "orphans" together for a hilarious luncheon and fashion swap. Each went home with fabulous finds, for free. The high-fashion red coat, the silver bracelet, the too-small cashmere sweater, of course, got snapped up—but so did the beach hat, the faded jeans, and the new ruffled apron.

The luncheon proved so successful that the idea caught on, as did guided tours to local thrift shops. In our city, smart ladies stay on the lookout, and alert one another to good finds—lined gray flannel slacks for twelve dollars, a Harris tweed jacket for thirty, a designer gown at one-third of last year's price. Hazel even found the gorgeous, longed-for crystal beads I'd wanted for twenty years—for just six dollars!

Discount houses, sales, consignment shops, friends' closets—there's fashion gold in them thar' places. As one minister's wife exhorted her circle group, "Ladies, there's no excuse for us to spend our husbands' money paying *retail.*"

Ingenuity, negotiation, thought. Anything you want or need can be produced—eventually—by those names. Meanwhile, let your friends know what you need and want. Organize a garage sale, swap meet, barter club, anything you like. Tell Mr. Jones you wish he'd paint your house, and suggest something you could do for him in exchange.

At the other end of the fiscal spectrum, there are those who need to simplify, cut back, bequeath, or bestow. "Too much property turned out to be a far worse problem than not enough," a physician said. "It took us a year to learn what our family needed, decide where we're headed, what we hoped for, and to undo our excesses.

"We sold our big house, two cars, and a vacation home. We moved into a simple but adequate condominium. I believe my wife and I will live much longer (I know we're far happier) because we're no longer serving *things.*"

• *Put yourself in charge.* Learn how to handle your money creatively, wisely, and well. Try some new thinking. Expand or contract, as you see fit. Above all, consider the words of Laura Sloate, financial manager, who said, "Health and money end up being the ruling principles of life. You may say you're not interested, but you can't live without them, and eventually you have to have some concern for both."

CHAPTER 7

Built to Last a Lifetime

Y our body is beautiful, and it's built to last. You can keep it beautiful: you can make it even *more* beautiful. Even if your body has become stiff, awkward, slowed down, or fat, you can decide to become slim, supple, and energetic. *At any age.* Talk about options!

As the psalmist wrote in Psalms 139:14, you are "fearfully and wonderfully made." (Just how wonderfully, scientists continue to discover, to our encouragement.) If your health is good, they say, you can make it better. If your health is poor, you can improve it radically. If you presently look, feel, and think *old,* you can opt to look, feel, and think *younger.* Much younger. *Even twenty or twenty-five years younger.*

Quite simply, researchers believe your life-style will determine the length and quality of your years. At the University of California at Los Angeles's Center for Health Enhancement, a longevity study, which followed some seven thousand people for a period of ten years, discovered *very* interesting relationships between life-style and longevity. People who practiced seven specific health habits were found to average *eleven additional years* of life beyond those who practiced none of them.

How is your life-style? The seven life-enhancing factors mentioned above include:

- Sleeping seven to eight hours a night

- Regular breakfast

- Keeping weight normal

- Occasional snacking only

- Regular vigorous exercise

- No smoking

- Moderate or no alcohol

If a 45-year-old man observes three of the above rules, the study shows he can expect to live to age 67. If he practices 6 or 7 of them, he can expect to live to 78.

How do you rate? If you scored less than perfect, why not challenge your family to an experiment? Make a game of it. Simply suggest that everyone abide by those seven simple rules for one month. For every rule broken each day, place a dime or a dollar (whatever you decide) into a kitty. Discuss your results at the end of the month. Help one another keep the rules. Use the money you collect for a fun purpose.

The goal? Creating new, good habits. If every family member gained one healthful habit, imagine the accrued results! Good health, as the above list shows, is mostly a matter of what our fathers termed "horse sense." Marjorie Holmes, the 70-year-old author of *God and Vitamins*, plus twenty other best-sellers, states it succinctly: "We are the food we eat, the water we drink, the air we breathe, and the thoughts we think."

Give yourself a health inventory. Simply place a check mark beside anything on the following list you'd rate *okay*. Place a cross mark beside anything you'd rate *needs improving or changing*. Here is the list:

- Eyesight (Do you need a checkup? New glasses?)

- Hearing

- Teeth (Due for a dental exam? Repairs? Cleaning?)

- Skin

- Muscle tone

- Weight

- Aerobic fitness

- Nonprescription drugs, such as aspirin

- Smoking

- Alcohol intake

Now, what are your personal goals? To decide, rate your cross marks. Which three items deserve top priority? What is your deadline for dental repair, an exercise program, or quitting smoking? Rate your top three items in order of importance, then handle them one at a time. Decide to begin. Decide to spend the time, money, and effort the job requires. You are worth it!

Suppose you attain those three health goals during the next twelve months. At that point, take another health inventory and work on another three important goals. You can see how attention and simple common sense literally can turn your health picture around. Your Super Years can abound with new vitality.

Simple as your health goals may be, however, you might find it difficult to begin; harder still to stick with it. Here are some ways to change your life-style and mean business about it. (After all, it's a matter of life or death.)

1. It's your life, and your decision to change. You are responsible for your own beautiful body.

2. Share your health goals with someone else. Ask for support and encouragement if you need it.

3. Don't try to change too many things too fast. One change at a time might be better.

4. Reward yourself when you succeed. Take credit for losing five pounds, going to bed earlier, or walking a mile. Brag on yourself a little!

5. Don't punish yourself when you fail. Just pick yourself up and start over. There's plenty of time.

6. Enjoy your successes. Become more aware of your body, your health, your energy. Enjoy yourself and everything about you.

After three years of illness and sedentary living, I decided to rebound to good health via an exercise trampoline (a minitrampoline designed for increasing aerobics fitness). My first session seemed disastrous—just sixty bounces, and my muscles turned to Jell-O and my breath gave out. "It's too little, too late," I gasped, heartbroken. "I'm over the hill!" From somewhere, a thought arrived: *Yes, but sixty bounces is better than nothing. What if I did that once an hour?*

Within a week, I could rebound for five minutes. By the end of that month I was up to ten. By that time, flabby muscles had begun to respond, deep breathing was rediscovered and prime time—good, hard *work* time—increased by a full two hours per day. Imagine my joy when, after four weeks, I discovered I'd lost *three inches.*

Delightful as all that might be, however, something far more important had occurred. I had discovered that so far as my body is concerned, *It's never too late.* It was there all the time, just waiting for me to reclaim it. And so is yours.

Your health story might become far more dramatic than mine. You could decide to increase your lung capacity, decrease your waistline, sing louder, dance longer, sleep sounder, laugh more, frown less, see farther, do better work, enjoy freer play, make love more often. . . .

Write your own ticket. Meanwhile, remember this: Our physical, mental, and emotional health depends on how we *eat, rest, and exercise.* Change one, two, or all three categories for the better, and your health can do a thrilling turnaround. "It's incredible," Dr. Charles Kleeman of the Center for Health Enhancement, Education and Research at UCLA observed, "that no matter what level of health individuals begin from, no matter what their age—when they start thinking about their health and become actively involved in a program of health enhancement, what positive changes can take place in as short a time as one month. I'm continually amazed."

Perhaps it's time for you to challenge yourself to become continually younger, healthier and better looking. You, like the American poet Longfellow, can determine that "joy, temperance, and repose, slam the door on the doctor's nose."

We have countless interesting models to follow. Gayelord Hauser, pioneer exponent of healthful living, cites the fascinating Lady Mendl, who was famous for standing on her head at age 80. Later she discovered the slant board, believed to be a wonderful asset to circulation, posture, musculature, and general health. Lady Mendl traded her headstands for the less dangerous slant board, which she used into her ninety-fourth year.

With or without a slant board, like Lady Mendl, you can take charge of your body and your life. You can decide to discover what works best for you, and stick with it. Some oldsters seem to break the rules and get away with it. George Burns, at 85, insisted, "There are no health rules with me. I don't go by the book. I don't listen to doctors either, unless I've got a pain or an ache. Doctors tell you not to smoke cigars and to take some exercise. . . .

"My health has been good. The only time I was really sick was when I was seventy-eight years old. I had triple bypass open-heart surgery. It was a big smash. It was so successful, it swept the country and now everybody's doing it."

Healthy, happy, and still hardworking, George Burns demonstrates yet another important health precept. He knows *laughter is still the best medicine!*

CHAPTER 8

Boosting Your Energy Quotient

ENERGY . . . vitality . . . super well-being. The longer you live, the better you *can* live, if you choose. Today, or any other day of your life, you can boost your energy level to a fantastic new high. You can open the door to enthusiasm. You can outwit killer stress. You can operate from intense new levels of satisfaction, joy, and general well-being.

"This world belongs to the energetic," Ralph Waldo Emerson opined. If you habitually equate energy with youth, think again. This world has begun to understand that *energy is ageless.* Anyone can energize himself at will.

Ruth Rothfarb, the world's oldest marathon runner, proves our point. At 80, Rothfarb finished the 26.2 mile Avon International at Ottawa, Canada, with a time of 5:39:46, making her the oldest woman ever to complete a marathon race. "I also saw her dance up a storm that same night, and she was still dancing when I left the postrace party at 10:30 that night," a witness said. "I am, after all, fifty-three years old, and I need my rest."

At age 72, Ruth Rothfarb started running. She had been a businesswoman all her life, and felt she needed a way to keep active. She noted that jogging seemed to help her arthritis. From there, it was a short eight-year trot to becoming a world-beater!

Inactivity ages the body, and inactivity ages the brain. "For the most part, age has become an irrelevant factor in terms of one's fitness level," reported Chris Silkwood, director of The Phoenix Spa in Houston, Texas. "I see women in their seventies outperform those in their thirties. It's a matter of your personal level of conditioning."

The Super Years, after all, are nothing new. Charles Dickens described one aspect vividly: "The wandering man knows of certain ancients, far gone in years, who have staved off infirmities and dissolution by earnest walking—hale fellows, close upon ninety, but brisk as boys."

What creates energy? Physical activity, of course—but also a very nonexotic potpourri of so many other life-producing, joy-giving factors! Consider these:

• *Laughter.* "Everybody ought to have a laughin' place," "Br'er Rabbit" believed. Where's yours? For Max Cleland, Georgia's secretary of state and former national administrator of the Veterans Administration, a television program called "Laugh In" became the most important "laughin' place" of his life, as he recovered from the loss of both legs and one arm during the Vietnam War. For Max Cleland and other seriously wounded men at Walter Reed Army Hospital in Washington, D.C., laughter became a strong brace in the bridge they crossed in order to regain full health.

Norman Cousins believes laughter restored his health, and has written two books concerning laughter and well-being. Desperately ill, with a prognosis of "incurable," Cousins determined to treat himself with laughter—jokes, "Candid Camera" reruns—anything he could find that proved humorous. Norman Cousins recovered, and scientists take his self-experiments seriously.

There is something restorative—some tonic medics respect but can't isolate—within laughter.

"Laughing is the sensation of feeling good all over, and showing it principally in one spot," said Josh Billings. Whatever it is, laughter produces immediate energy, as any real laugher knows.

"The laughter of man is the contentment of God," John Weiss believed. And H. W. Shaw (also known as Josh Billings) took it further: "Morally considered, laughter is next to the Ten Commandments."

Check your own laugh quotient. Does your giggle still gurgle? Is there glee in your guffaw? As some people age, their laugh gets rustier and rustier, like the hinge on a sagging gate. Perhaps they need a "Hee-Haw" prescription, or a trip through some *New Yorker* magazine cartoons.

Remember to laugh. It's free as a Humane Society kitten. It's a real pep pill (likely to be habit forming). Actually, laughter *could* save your life!

• *Sleep and Rest.* "Sleep is a barometer of your physical and mental well-being," says Dr. Quentin Regestein, director of the sleep clinic of Boston's Peter Brent Brigham Hospital and Assistant Professor of Psychiatry at Harvard Medical School. "You need sleep to feel your best."

As you know, a sleep deficit quickly drains your energy reserves. You *deserve* that eight-hour sleep tonight. It's still a staple in your energy diet. In fact, fewer than six hours or more than nine hours' sleep was associated with a higher mortality rate and bad health, according to the California longevity study mentioned earlier.

There's a lot you can do to produce good sleep for yourself.

Boost your energy through abundant rest and sleep. Check these simple suggestions from Dr. Regestein:

- Maintain a regular bedtime.

- Keep your bedroom quiet and below 75 degrees.

- Never take sleeping pills, if possible. They do not produce normal sleep, and eventually can result in insomnia.

- Don't exercise too near bedtime, or eat heavy food.

- Give your central nervous system a break. Cigarettes, alcohol, over-the-counter sleep inducers, large amounts of coffee, cola, or tea all inhibit sleep.

- Check your bed, mattress, and pillow. Make sure they're comfortable and supportive.

- Know your body. Pace yourself. Take fifteen-minute or half-hour catnaps if you're a sixteen-hour, nonstop person.

"At least half the people who consult me about spiritual problems could solve them easily if they'd just get a good night's sleep," one minister says. Think of L'il Abner, the comic page hillbilly, who got a job as a mattress tester. Or consider the words of Leigh Hunt:

> It is a delicious moment, certainly, that of being well nestled in bed and feeling that you shall drop gently to sleep. The good is to come, not past; the limbs are tired enough to render the remaining in one posture delightful; the labor of the day is gone.
> A gentle failure of the perceptions creeps over you; the spirit of consciousness disengages itself once more, and with slow and

hushing degrees, like a mother detaching her hand from that of a sleeping child, the mind seems to have a balmy lid closing over it, like the eye—it is closed—the mysterious spirit has gone to take its airy rounds.

Read that, and sleep tight!

• *Eating Habits.* Your Super Years depend upon how well you fuel yourself. Today is the day to plan your weight, your teeth and bones, quality of skin, hair, eyesight, and everything else that depends upon body nourishment.

According to Chris Silkwood, the important basic concepts remain few and simple. Choose *complex* carbohydrates—fruits, grains, and vegetables—for at least 50 percent of your food intake. Avoid *simple* carbohydrates—refined sugars and starches that offer little more than empty calories.

Eat *lean* protein—fish, skinned chicken or turkey, and very little red meat. Choose skim or low-fat dairy proteins.

Fats should be *unsaturated* vegetable fats, and a very small percentage of your diet.

Drink water. If you're not already conscientious about water consumption, trying drinking eight tall glasses a day for just one week. You'll experience an amazing release from fatigue, definite feelings of well-being. Try water. It's free. It's tremendously beneficial.

Find some caffeine substitutes. Cut back on coffee, tea, and cola drinks—or cut them out entirely—and watch your energy increase. Perhaps you're addicted to caffeine. If leaving off coffee produces the jitters, a low-grade headache, or a mean mood, face yourself honestly. Which means more to you: your caffeine habit, or a new bounce in your step?

How important are the simple rules we list here? Again, you really are what you eat. Erratic eaters, according to the California longevity study, suffered much worse health than those who ate three regular meals a day. Eating breakfast has a particular value, it was shown.

Study your eating habits. Will they carry you into your Super Years at a really super pace? "I knew all that coffee I was drinking was bad for my nerves," Wanda confessed. "Then I read somewhere that too much caffeine could cause premature gray hair. *That* did it! It wasn't all that hard to cut back to two cups a day."

• *Exercise.* ". . . exercise is a necessity, to be done without fail, even if, like brushing one's teeth, one does it alone," wrote Isadore Rossman, M.D., Ph.D., in his foreword to *Sixty-Plus and Fit Again,* by Magda Rosenberg. "As Mrs. Rosenberg points out," he continues, "only a few minutes a day are all that is needed to maintain fitness and prevent atrophy in senior citizens.

"A few minutes a day seems like a small investment for a rich return. A regular exercise program gives a sense of well-being in the present, and it also gives the older person a reserve of strength to call upon if the need arises. From the viewpoint of the physician, this physical reserve in a patient, especially an older one, can be critical: it may determine whether one becomes bedbound or bounces back after a fracture, an operation, a bout of the flu. Many experiences in this area have convinced me of the value of exercise."

Look around you. The exercise craze has caught on, gained ground, and everywhere you go, you see magnificent results. Young, old, in-between, Americans understand how easy it is to improve the quality of life, simply by *using the body.* Everything improves with use. Your body, properly used, can please you more now and for all the other years of your life.

"... A few minutes of exercise a day can mean the difference between an unhappy and dependent old age, and later years that are full of pleasure and activity—and usefulness," writes Magda Rosenberg. "Only minutes a day, every day, can turn a healthy senior citizen who has succumbed to a sedentary life into an active, vigorous human being who can prove to the world that old age does not mean the end of living."

Dr. Kenneth Cooper, in his classic exercise book entitled *Aerobics,* says, "Medical research has given us new insight into the process of aging. Aging is accelerated by inactivity. Lack of exercise seems to be a major factor in premature aging."

The fantastic energizing powers inherent within even the simplest exercise disciplines have been well documented. Your Super Years begin *today,* if you decide to join the exercise bunch. At home, beside the TV, at the YMCA, the office, your apartment clubhouse, retirement homes, church gymnasiums—join in!

As Magda Rosenberg promises, "... backs don't have to ache, legs don't have to be weak. Life doesn't have to be a tedious, lonely existence because of physical impairment. You don't have to sit in a chair alone at home, an object of pity to your offspring, someone's unwanted responsibility."

And in case you think, as I did, that for *your* body it's too late: "Age has nothing to do with it. Our muscles don't know the difference between young and old."

Get out and *move it.* That surge of new power you'll feel ... why, that's the *real you!*

• *Stress Relievers.* Relieve small stresses in your life: release new energy! Just for fun, take a small survey right now. See any obvious energy leaks you can plug up? The minor irritants, hassles and small things that "bend you out of shape" do add up. These suggestions could help:

1. Take time for yourself.

2. Confront what's bothering you.

3. Make exercise a treat, not a treatment.

4. How about a massage?

5. Write FUN on your calendar.

6. Tell someone you love him/her.

7. Express concern.

8. Run away from home for an hour or two.

9. Say *no* when you need to.

10. Write things down.

11. Prepare for tomorrow tonight.

12. Take something to do while you wait.

13. Simplify.

14. Laugh more.

15. Don't do too many hateful chores in one day.

16. Forgive, then forgive again.

17. Look good when you leave the house.

18. Buy a small safe in which to keep scissors, money for the paperboy, adhesive tape, stamps and other important items the family appropriates.

The point is, make your own list. *You* know what distresses you. *You* know what drives you crazy. Determine to drive small problems out of your life. Release your energies for the big accomplishments and big pleasures you deserve to enjoy.

"Stress is cumulative," psychologist and stress expert Ken Dychtwald said. "The older you get, the more likely it is that stress is going to show up."

De-fuse that dynamite. Take preventive measures against stress buildup in your life. Determine to find answers for the problems that deplete your precious energy stores. "City traffic drove me crazy," Ken said. "I could feel my blood pressure rise during all that rush-hour, start-stop stuff. I knew I couldn't take it indefinitely.

"I decided to go to work two hours earlier every day. By the time everybody else gets there, I've got a load of work done. I leave early each afternoon, before the traffic gets heavy, and early enough to work in the yard. Why didn't I think of that years ago?"

Not everyone can change his work hours that way, but the point is—Ken found a solution for his stress problem. So can you!

• *Change Your Pace.* A simple trick, but for some reason it works—just change your pace. If you're pushed, rushed and exhausted, deliberately slow down to a crawl for a day or a week. If you're presently operating at a moderate or slow speed, gear up. Something about resetting your internal "cruise control" results in a new surge of energy.

Another hint: Get up one or two hours earlier. Oh, not forever—just for tomorrow, or for the rest of this week. You'll feel smart, stimulated, and on top of the world.

You can learn ways to generate new energy—not just for this day, but for the rest of your life. Try it. Think of ways to make it happen. Didn't you always have a certain amount of built-in TNT?

If you're the young man who hit the longest fly balls in town—who once helped place Dr. Black's Chevrolet atop the Administration Building—or marched twenty miles a day in the Infantry. . . .

If you're the young woman who could dance all night—scrub the whole house by nine o'clock in the morning—or teach thirty six-year-olds, then come home to your own husband and kids. . . .

You *know* God gave you great energy. If you've lost it, go find it again. You'll need it for your Super Years!

CHAPTER 9

Facing Forward

Y<small>OUR</small> Super Years! You anticipate them. You imagine yourself, you picture your partner—and the future seems to shine with promise. You're facing forward, and it's exciting. Moreover, as you consider the multifaceted Self you're learning to appreciate, you're pleased by the priceless intangibles you've gained—poise, experience, gentleness, self-confidence, optimism. . . .

You like what you see. Truly, such self-esteem enriches not just your present, but your Super Years. The longer you live, in fact, the more essential it becomes—*a clear and loving self-image.*

The Reverend Robert H. Schuller, pastor of the Crystal Cathedral in California and of the "Hour of Power" television ministry, believes self-esteem to be nothing less than the "divine dignity that God intended to be our emotional birthright as children created in His image."

A study conducted by the Gallup poll organization shows that people with firm self-esteem are healthier, happier, and more productive than those without it. Lack of such esteem, Schuller says, causes many of us to fear problems and hold doubts about the future.

How much do you enjoy your physical image? Your face? Hair? Posture? Hands? The way you walk, talk, smile, and laugh? Are you good-looking? Do others love to watch you?

Psychologists agree that your outside says a lot about your inside. Psychology professor Ellen Berscheid, Ph.D., asserts that pretty people are more likely to achieve greater success than plain people. Tests showed that attractive people were perceived as persons of greater warmth, sensitivity, kindness, and modesty, she wrote in *Psychological Aspects of Facial Form.*

Doctor Berscheid's work also supports another provocative idea: as people move frequently, often far from family and friends, *first impressions and physical appearance become crucially important.*

Joanne Wallace, nationally known image authority, agrees. "When people meet for the first time, an impression is left—if it is pleasing, there will be further contact. If it is displeasing, it can mean the end of a potential friendship," she writes in *Dress With Style.* Mrs. Wallace, president and founder of Image Improvement, Inc., and author of *Image of Loveliness,* wrote: "You are a custom-made individual, created unique with your very own beautiful color palette of hair, eyes, and skin tone, designed with your own physical frame, and ready to develop your own personal style."

Gloria Vanderbilt, artist, designer, and author, calls beauty and health "reflections of a woman's mind and her soul. As simply as I can express it, a beautiful woman, a person, radiates from within. Each woman works from an ideal image that she constantly carries with her and that she constantly strives to recreate day after day...."

Some men seem to carry an ideal image, also. George Burns, still a hardworking show-biz personality at age 87, invariably projects a refined style enhanced by personal flair. Two years ago an interviewer described Burns's appearance. "As always, he was nattily dressed in immaculately tailored sports jacket and slacks. He wore an expensive open shirt."

Burns made some trenchant comments about age and image. "A lot of people get to be seventy and think they're supposed to be old," he said. "So they start to practice being old.

"They walk slow, they talk slow. They get up slow and they sit down slow. It takes them twenty minutes to get out of the car. They spill food on themselves.

"With all that practice, by the time they're seventy-five years old, they're now a success. They're now old. Not me. I'm a failure. I don't practice."

Like others successfully enjoying their Super Years, a George Burns or a Gloria Vanderbilt bears a distinct aura, a well-defined personality that appears to become more finely etched with each season that passes. So much of their charisma is physical, because their physical selves continually communicate.

"We are all sculptors and painters, and our material is our own flesh and blood and bones," Thoreau wrote. And Emerson paralleled the thought: "There are faces so fluid with expression, so flushed and rippled by the play of thought, that we can hardly find what the mere features really are.

"When the delicious beauty of lineaments loses its power," he continued, "it is because a more delicious beauty has appeared— that an interior and durable form has been disclosed."

What do your face and body communicate? How much of beauty or elegance, life and health, fun and style? What do you *desire* to communicate? Do your eyes speak? Emerson once wrote, "Some eyes have no more expression than blueberries, while others are as deep as a well which you can fall into."

You can learn to like your looks. You can learn how to express your Self via your face, eyes, and body. You can communicate whatever you are, freely and unself-consciously. Take your Self into your Super Years—*your whole Self.* As Joanne Wallace writes in *Dress With Style,* "It's never too late to change—never too late to improve your image. . . .

"An ageless person looks capable, dynamic, vital, healthy, and contemporary. She updates her hair, her makeup, her clothes, *everything.* She reads books and magazines and becomes an expert on herself. She doesn't copy other women who may be confused about their images. She wears what becomes *her.*"

Gloria Vanderbilt speaks to the power of supportive friends as a source of energy she believes in. "One must have supportive images throughout life," she said. "Who we select as friends, who we gravitate towards has important consequences to our abilities to create, love, enjoy and share. I'm for having life-enhancing friends near whenever I can. They're the ones beauty can happen with."

Beauty can and should increase, year by year. Your beauty should last throughout your lifetime. Recently Ella Marsh Adams, my neighbor, took me to visit her 101-year-old friend Mrs. Abbie Busbee. I'd heard a great deal about Abbie—her delightful mind, the fact that she'd worked until age 83, then retired to mind children for another several years—but nothing I heard prepared me for the fact of Abbie herself.

"You're beautiful!" I blurted out, the moment I met her.

"Thank you, dear," she smiled, sitting as erect in her wheelchair as a queen on her throne.

Abbie Busbee unnerved me completely. As we chatted and interviewed, I kept sneaking peeks. Her face, so unexpectedly lovely, has the fine bone structure and delicate skin for which

Georgia belles are famous—but *that skin looks virtually unlined.*

The ladies worked on a guest list for Abbie's forthcoming birthday party. As the birthday girl sorted out names, I watched the slender, perfectly manicured hands turn pages of the address book—hands as young and wrinkle-free as Abbie's face. Her eyes, clear and china blue, flashed and sparkled when she was amused—and it amused her some, that Ella Marsh and I kept taking our reading glasses off and putting them on. *Abbie doesn't need glasses.*

That perfect, porcelain complexion . . . the graceful hands . . . the finishing-school posture . . . her aureole of platinum hair . . . the firm voice, sprightly conversation and sense of humor . . . those blue eyes any woman in the world might envy . . . undeniably, Abbie Busbee is gorgeous.

I put down my notepad and faced her. "What in the world do you do for your face?" I demanded.

"I put castor oil on my face every night, and also rub it into my hands. It soaks in, where most oils stay on top of the skin," she explained. "I've watched a little too much TV lately, and it's made some fine wrinkles around my eyes. I put a little extra oil there. . . ."

"Just castor oil?" I stared. Then I thought of the obvious answer. "You must have done this all your life?" *No wonder,* I thought, *if you've taken such good care of your skin for one hundred years. . . .*

She shook her head and laughed. "No, I didn't hear about this until I was eighty. Just try it, honey. I do believe you'll like it!"

I picked up the notepad again. "Any beauty tips for the woman who is aging? Anything you'd do differently if you could go back?"

"Yes, indeed," came the instantaneous reply. "I'd take better care of my teeth. I didn't *dream* I'd live this long, and I had to get dentures at age eighty-seven."

In California, where Vi Shoemaker Shattuck teaches Image Improvement classes, a *grande dame* named Ethel Ziegler Hicks enrolled. "She heard me say Image Improvement is for women of all ages, nine to ninety," Vi explained, "and Ethel replied, 'I'm ninety-one and one-half.'

"Interested in meeting people and improving herself, she attended all the classes and did every assignment. Ethel enjoyed the color analysis, wardrobe coordination, hairstyles ... the whole thing. She's a very classy lady with lots of strength. She had terrific style as it was, but she could learn still more!"

You can have ageless beauty. "In all ranks of life the human heart yearns for the beautiful," wrote Harriet Beecher Stowe, "and the beautiful things that God makes are his gift to all alike."

You'll find new worlds of beauty suggestions aimed toward the Super Years. New thinking includes these tips:

• *Gray Hair.* "Gray hair should be glorious, sparkling, bright like platinum," says premier haircolorist Leslie Blanchard. The coloring expert recommends periodic wardrobe and makeup assessment as hair grays, focusing on blues and bright colors to offset potentially draining effects of gray hair.

• *Men and Thinning Hair.* If you're one of the six out of ten men who show signs of thinning hair, you'll want to know about a system which includes shampoo, rinse, treatment, and finishing spray. Baldness can't be averted, but hair can look fuller and become easier to control.

• *Color Analysis.* Women *and* men benefit from color analysis, which types you by season of the year, so you can choose wardrobe and other colors most flattering to you. Whether you are an Autumn, Winter, Spring or Summer, there's a range of colors which invariably enhances your hair, eyes, skin and personality type. Joanne Wallace's *Dress With Style* explains fully how you can dramatize your looks by proper color selection.

• *Perhaps you need a fashion consultant.* If you doubt your own taste, or wonder if you should change "looks" as you get older, find a consultant to help you. Men as well as women enjoy an outside opinion on the look, the lines, the message an outfit conveys. This help need not be expensive. Often a YWCA or other community organization offers fashion classes or individual consultation. It's a great way to update!

• *Hairstyling.* This can be had at low cost or sometimes even free, if you know how to find it. Beauty schools and barber schools offer a full range of services, carefully supervised and performed by well-trained students, at very reasonable prices. In larger cities, check the *Personal* classification in your newspaper's classified ads. Often master beauticians or barbers need models. It's a good way to receive an excellent new style for free.

Joanne Wallace says:

> It's important to present a look that says to the world that you care about your body, posture, makeup, and hair. . . . Pay attention to what makes you feel good about yourself.
>
> Not so long ago, forty was over the hill, and fifty was old. Now, with marvelous research in skin and cosmetic products, it's possible to look attractive and energetic at any age.

Sir James M. Barrie described charm, which is a kind of beauty, as "a sort of bloom on a woman. If you have it you don't need to have anything else; and if you don't have it, it doesn't much matter what else you have."

Man or woman, *each* can extend his own personal beauty throughout the Super Years. Gloria Vanderbilt exhorts us all:

I believe very strongly that one of the most revolutionary aspects of this century has been to make beauty and health available to everyone. American women are constantly involved in self-improvement. I'm proud of my age and the experience that has come with it. I'm not interested in looking younger than I am, but I also feel that I would take steps to look vital.

... Age, change, and wisdom do not come easily for women—or for men. But as I see it—ripeness is all!

CHAPTER 10

The Adventure Club

CHARTER your own adventure club! Ten years ago an Atlanta attorney did just that. Hamilton Lokey and his wife, Muriel, formed the Adventure Club that year on her birthday. The purpose? Its members "were to have adventures," Lokey explained. So far the two-member club (sometimes they admit another couple or two) has climbed Mount Fuji, Mount Rainier and Mount Kilimanjaro. They have traveled the Inca Trail and ventured into Tibet.

At 71, "Ham" Lokey—with his agile and adventurous wife— has plenty to share, via public lectures and slide shows. The Adventure Club has taken its membership to places many of us dream of visiting, but would consider too tough to conquer. "I might climb two or three flights of stairs—but only if it were a really *top flight* resort hotel," one lady remarked dubiously. "That's plenty of adventure for me!"

The astonishing idea of regular *adventure*—that is, adventure as a normal and planned-for component of life—seems never to occur to some people. Test yourself. If you decided to choose an adventure, what would you choose? Where would you go? What would you do? When would you begin? I decided to ask five people those questions.

"Easy. I'd travel to Israel and live in a kibbutz for one year," a man responded. "No, I couldn't go for at least five years, until my son could handle my business. Then I could go, but I imagine I really wouldn't be up to it by that time."

Adventure or fantasy? Many don't know the difference. People I questioned offered ideas ranging from living in a log cabin and photographing wild flowers to panning for gold, or living in a houseboat. Not one person actually planned to implement his dreams. All dismissed their ideas as "foolish," "impractical," or "immature." Each admitted his adventure *could* be attained, *but*. . . .

Not everyone needs adventure, of course. Some frenetic individuals cry out for the opposite, in fact; their lives lack sameness, routine and/or stability, and they long for a calm period. Most of us, however, experience an itch to do at least one inexplicable feat, see one longed-for destination, or try one mad idea before we die. As Antoine Lemierre wrote, "It is a profound mistake to think that everything has been discovered; as well think the horizon the boundary of the world."

How can you discover what it is you really hope to discover? Even if you are adventurous, how do you pin down *the* adventure? And how far can you really afford to let your imagination rip? Ask yourself: *If I had my life to live over, what things would I do?*

Nadine Stair, an 85-year-old Louisville, Kentucky woman, answered this way:

If I had my life to live over, I'd dare to make more mistakes next time. I'd relax, I would limber up. I would be sillier than I have been this trip. I would take fewer things seriously. I would take more chances. I would climb more mountains and swim more rivers. I would eat more ice cream and less beans. I would perhaps have more actual troubles, but I'd have fewer imaginary ones.

You see, I'm one of those people who live sensibly and sanely hour after hour, day after day. Oh, I've had my moments, and if I had to do it over again, I'd have more of them. In fact, I'd try to have nothing else. Just moments, one after another, instead of living so many years ahead of each day. I've been one of those persons who never goes anywhere without a thermometer, a hot-water bottle, a raincoat and a parachute. If I had to do it again, I would travel lighter than I have.

If I had my life to live over, I would start barefoot earlier in the spring and stay that way later in the fall. I would go to more dances. I would ride more merry-go-rounds. I would pick more daisies.

What if you had your life to live over? Well, in a sense, you do. Life begins all over again with every sunrise. Further, if you want adventure—it's *yours.* "The more we do, the more we can do; the more busy we are, the more leisure we have," William Hazlitt, English writer, encouraged.

Play around with the idea of adventure. (Not every Adventure Club member must climb mountains to qualify!) Put your imagination into gear and consider the following:

• *Charter your own Adventure Club.* Decide its purpose, and who you'll invite to join. Is it a travel club? Book club? Idea group?

Can you meet around your kitchen table, or should you hire a hall? Will you be democratic, or very, very exclusive? Who do you know who *invites* adventures to happen?

• *Decide to widen a narrow life or focus a scattered one.* Do you *always* choose vanilla? Drive home from work the same way? Do the same things each Saturday at the same time, with the same friends?

Or, do you *never* have plans? Nap on Saturday evening because you didn't think about going to the movie until too late? Do you skip vacations? Does Christmas always catch you by surprise?

Either way, you could use some stirring up! Dream up something new and different you could do. Think who'd be your absolutely best partner in adventure. Give yourself five minutes to dream up a fabulous plot, another five to sell it to someone else. Ten minutes from now, you could be packing for Rio! Adventure is like that, you know.

• *Choose a few friends who can expand you.* Look around for those who think opposite of you. Deliberately ask someone "not your type" to work, plan, or play with you. Try to get into new grooves, for a change, or onto the wavelengths of people very different from those you usually choose. It's mind stretching and exciting!

• *Begin to strengthen your present relationships.* These are the friends, your "chosen people," you'll take with you through life—wife or husband, cousin, college roommate, army buddy. These are the ones you love the deepest and best—the comfortable ones you can take for granted.

Don't. Instead of taking for granted, make this a year for special treats. Dream up something unforgettable, unique, maybe even romantic. For her fifty-third birthday in 1976, President Reagan gave his Nancy a fifteen-foot canoe, the *TruLuv,* paddled her out into the middle of a lake on their California estate, and serenaded her.

When John flew to Chicago for three weeks of training, Judy knew he'd be homesick. She phoned their friends and assigned two dozen letters, notes, or phone calls spaced, so he'd experience at least one surprise per day. "It was like a surprise party strung out over three weeks," Judy explained. "We all got a kick out of it. John still can't believe it!"

Margaret spent a month in Florida when her mother needed help following a bad fall. Returning home tired and anxious, Margaret was thrilled to discover that Joe had painted their bedroom lilac. "Simple," Joe admitted modestly. "I figured you'd pick up a color from the flowers in the draperies. *Then* I figured you'd pick that sissy lavender!"

Lilac or not, it's fun to think of ways to give those we love a real jolt of joy. Venture out. Show that you're an appreciator. Be willing to risk. Put new adventure in those old, tried-and-true relationships.

• *Do something outrageous.* Spend your life's savings on a piano for your daughter. Take your family to a whole day of movies—four in a row. Come home from work early and drive fifty miles down the road to dinner; then take the long way home, holding hands, and watching the moon glow.

Spend a whole day in bed. Read a book, polish your fingernails, reread your love letters, plan a party—even doze, if you like.

One woman has a Chocolate Soda Club, formed when she was in her teens. Bylaws are simple: just find a friend (or more) and partake of a real, old-fashioned stem-winder of a chocolate soda. The occasion arises just once a year, and must be totally spontaneous. If the friend protests about calories, one must be kind but firm, steering him or her into the soda parlor with a strong grip and ordering for the shaken one: one scoop of chocolate, one of vanilla, extra whipped cream, and a cherry. Accept no substitutes!

• *Plan for life alone.* All adventures are not pure fun. Life can change with agonizing swiftness. Sometimes one receives news that cramps the heart, that limits even unspoken plans. Nobody, after all, plans to become widowed.

However, we should. At least, it makes sense to think what we would do should we ever suddenly find ourselves living alone— regardless of the reason—with little or no warning or preparation. Prepare today. Simply ask yourself, "How would I choose to live and what would I do if ——— were not here?" A painful question, yes, but today it's only theoretical. How much better to think through the ramifications of the unthinkable *now;* then tuck away the mental answers against that day in which they might be needed.

"I know how Frank feels about the family business, and how hard he's worked to build it," a wife remarked. "Three years ago it dawned on me that if anything happened to my husband, I'd have to sell everything he's devoted himself to creating. For three years now I've come to the plant every Friday, and Frank shows me something, or has an employee explain some phase of operation.

"This gives us a chance to have lunch together, too. I've learned a lot, not just about Frank's business but also about his thinking. He knows that if I had to run this business, I'd know what he'd want me to do. This has brought us much closer together."

• *Begin today.* These are your Super Years, and you can fill them with adventure. Ready? If so, consider these ideas:

1. *Choose a partner for your adventure.* Edith selects a grand-child, sometimes two, to accompany her to a dude ranch, formal reception, or baseball game. Not only does she enjoy each of the

youngsters (she reports that all eight seem to be unusually gifted and charming), but she attempts to enlarge their fund of experiences.

2. *Build a support group.* Bring people into your life who offer some real "up" time. Choose some new friends who like you and love to say so, who boost your spirits, who affirm you in every way. Tough times come to us all. The friends around us provide the love that helps us tough it out. Who would you want around you at a time like that?

3. *Start a diary.* Record changes in your thoughts, feelings, and plans. Take note of the surprises and serendipities, the mads and glads, the people and places that impress you most. You're writing something important—personal and family history!

There's adventure awaiting you. It's around the corner, in the next room, or possibly it's lurking in your heart. Plan for it. Scheme a little. Today, seek something a little new and different—something fresh and surprising—and *super* special.

Above all, *your* adventure should have your name on it. *Your* spirit should ignite the whole idea. *Your* signature should stamp it as valid.

Be open to adventure. Dare to enrich your Super Years!

CHAPTER 11

Cures for Common Loneliness

It's *very* common—that aching, dejected form of solitude we call "loneliness." Rich or poor, popular or neglected, young or old, none of us manages to escape that peculiar sickness of the soul. Evangelist Billy Graham says loneliness has become the world's most widespread disease.

Who knows a cure for loneliness? Do you? *The quality of your Super Years depends upon your finding it.*

A newspaper columnist printed a lighthearted complaint about the burden of attending too many Christmas parties. In response, a reader wrote, ". . . I am sixty years old and never have attended a party in my life. I don't have even one friend. . . ."

How can that be? the newswriter wondered. How could someone literally have not one friend? Is that possible? Whether or not her idea is factual, obviously the reader *believes* herself to be friendless. Perhaps you identify with her feelings. You may have known heartbreaking loneliness in the past, or you may feel it now. Almost certainly, however, you know—or will know—someone else who feels just that desolate.

It's important to deal with loneliness before it happens—or at least before it becomes acute. "The only way to have a friend is to be one," Emerson wrote. Simplistic advice, perhaps, but as often as we've heard it, nevertheless it remains true. *Head loneliness off at the pass. Be someone's friend.*

Interestingly, the lady who wrote to the columnist failed to supply a return address. The newswriter responded in a follow-up column, but had no way to send a personal reply. Why no address? Was it pure oversight, or a dread of being contacted? By omitting her return address, how many letters and offers of friendship did the suffering woman deflect?

Strange to say, many of us behave much like the lonely woman. We reach out, yet leave no space for response. Still, the answer for which we yearn *always* is there, if we'll just allow it. "No one [is] so utterly desolate," Longfellow wrote, "but some heart, though unknown, responds unto his own."

Most news reporters can vouch for that. Whenever a story about loneliness, fear, or any other sort of human need is published, a tide of letters and phone calls results. Our nation numbers millions of concerned and caring hearts. Most Americans remain ready to reach out in love.

There's plenty of love for you. Think of that, when you feel painfully solitary. There's companionship for you. There's interesting work, laughter, stimulating ideas, jokes, and sound friendships. There are hugs for you, too, plus kisses and squeezes. *You need to be touched.* (That's a scientific fact, you know. It's believed that each of us requires some fourteen touches per day for optimal emotional health!)

Rather than become candidates for terminal loneliness, we need to continually build a support system about us. We need other people, other ideas. We need reenforcement; we also need to give to others. Like Charlie Brown in the "Peanuts" comic strips, we must declare, "I need all the friends I can get."

Here are some ways to gain friends and combat loneliness:

• *Be your own best friend.* The Greek philosopher Pythagoras said, "Above all things, reverence yourself." True self-respect means you can enjoy your own thoughts, ideas, and whimsies. You can eat, sing, play and laugh alone, on occasion. Writer Katherine Mansfield described self-friendship delightfully:

> I really only have Perfect Fun with myself. Other people won't stop and look at the things I want to look at or, if they do, they stop to please me or to humor me or to keep the peace.

Venture out alone, and if you're enjoying yourself, you inevitably meet at least one stranger who becomes a friend. Alone, you can do things you'd otherwise be too self-conscious to do before others—like trying on all the hats in the Straw Market.

Try an experiment. Take yourself out (anywhere at all will do) and enjoy yourself to the limit. Treat yourself to a bowling game, a hot-fudge sundae, a concert, or an art exhibit, or a dog show—and see who pops up. I'd be so surprised if you returned home without at least one interesting new friend that I'll actually wager you (*sh-h-h*) a big, chocolate soda!

• *Act.* Before those little "blue" feelings develop, before depression occurs, check to see if you're lonely. Perhaps you've worked too hard lately. Maybe you're stale from too little physical activity. Or are you tense or worried? Do you need a laughin' place?

Diagnose your loneliness, then act promptly. If you're tired and stiff, ask your neighbor to join you for a walk. (Choose a brisk, long-legged neighbor, however, if you want the walk to mean anything.) For laughter, take a child to a funny movie. For sheer hilarity, you can't beat a Disney shaggy-dog story, matinee performance, with two hundred moppets filling the theater with genuine belly laughs.

Or perhaps you need stimulus. "It is good to rub and polish our brain against that of others," French writer Montaigne wrote. Some days we need to visit our friend's art studio, take someone to see a Shakespeare play, or simply invite to lunch the brainiest, most absorbingly interesting conversationalist you know. You get lonely for *ideas*. An hour or two with a real idea person almost amounts to a shot of adrenalin.

• *Balance your life.* Too much sickness, work, or unrelieved responsibility can create loneliness that's hard to overcome. Consciously attempt to balance alone-time with public-time, work with play, inside with outside. Sometimes we're not so much lonely as just plain *dull.*

"I'd become full of resentment," Jan confessed. "After nursing Mother through two heart attacks, which I was privileged to do, I found myself feeling totally out-of-touch with others. Before I could reenter my own world, I had to face the fact that I resented the fact that I'd left it at all—even for Mother's sake.

"I was lonely because I was petulant. I wanted my friends to return to *me*. I expected them to read my mind, to show up when I wanted them to. Finally I realized what I was doing. I phoned a few people, expressed gratitude for Mother's restored health, then told each one that I was about to die from loneliness. That's all it took! My feelings of grief and depression left me that same day."

• *Start your life over.* Death, divorce, a move to a distant city or even a new community—these mileposts invariably create loneliness. Grief work takes time. Physical settling following a move takes time. After that, however, we need to do as Jan did—decide to start over.

In *Dag Hammarskjöld: Strictly Personal, A Portrait* by Bo Beskow, the author relates:

> Our fathers both died that year, and I could well understand Dag's feeling of being free to be himself. Starting on a new life means cutting old strings and school-ties and making new friends. Having met at this turning point had something to do with our continued friendship.

The Super Years will be punctuated by fresh starts. I must decide to engineer a way out of loneliness, and that decision, that method, resides within me. In *To Live Again,* Catherine Marshall's poignant account of Dr. Peter Marshall's untimely death and her dealings with widowhood, Catherine describes her own start over:

> Day after day that first summer I found that my journey through the Valley was a running battle with self-pity. . . . Try as I might to overcome it, I would find that being in the presence of couples threw my aloneness into sharpest perspective. . . .
>
> What then is the solution? It must lie somewhere in the realm of relationship. As solitaries we wither and die. We long to be needed; we yearn to be included; we thirst to know that we belong to someone. The question is . . . how can we achieve that sense of belonging?
>
> There is a price to be paid. The first tribute exacted is a modicum of honesty with ourselves. Do we so want to be rid of self-pity that we will allow ourselves no more wallowing in loneliness? How badly do we want to make connection with other people? Do we really want to find happiness again?
>
> In the light of honest answers to questions like these, suddenly we find that we do not ever need to be lonely, unless we choose to

be. For there are always others eager to receive our friendship if only we will take the first steps out of our solitary shell.

• *Walk through some new doors.* New community or old home-town, it's safe to suppose you have little idea of all the fascinating groups and associations waiting to welcome you. Ready to explore? With pen and paper, your telephone directory's Yellow Pages, and perhaps a spouse or friend, look up the following and list the ones that interest you:

1. Churches

2. Clubs and lodges

3. Associations

4. Health clubs

5. Social agencies

Should you live in a large city, it will take an evening just to sort out the possibilities. Even in a small town, there's a breath-taking potential for purposeful answers to your loneliness.

Choose two or three organizations that interest you most. Telephone immediately. Ask questions. Request information or brochures.

No more loneliness! Suddenly you're signed up for beginning ski lessons, the African violet show, or membership at the *Y.* You're ready to meet new people. You're available to offer friendship.

"It makes me sick, though," Barbara remarked. "There's so much to do that's interesting, and I can only choose two or three. It's an embarrassment of riches!"

One evening Don and Helen discussed their need for some new

faces in their lives. "Too many of our friends are just our age," Don observed. "I think we should diversify."

Soon the couple agreed to sponsor an international student, providing hospitality and a home-away-from-home for a full school year. How they enjoyed tall, blond Klaus! Too soon, however, he returned to his home in Germany, leaving Don and Helen feeling bereft. A year later, the couple decided to visit Klaus's parents in Germany. This summer, their visit will be reciprocated.

"How much that conversation with Helen widened our world," Don reflected. "We've begun to explore our desires and hopes and some possibilities, and to find ways to keep life interesting.

"We took Klaus because we were lonely for young people, needing to experience a young person's thinking and viewpoint. Klaus and his friends made our whole house jump, at times. But why not? After all, we're young folks too!"

• *Physical impairment need not create loneliness.* Jessie Hickford was past fifty when she became totally blind. At first, she found it nearly impossible to accept her new limitations. Then she decided to apply for a guide dog—and Prudence led her to new freedom and independence. She wrote in *Jessie Hickford: I Never Walked Alone:*

> I wanted to offer accommodation to a widowed friend, and as she had two grown-up children living at home it meant that we would need four bedrooms whereas my little house had only three. At first I thought of having the detached garage at the side of the house joined on to the building and converted into a ground-floor bedroom for myself, but I was advised to do more than this.
>
> I was reminded that I was an independent, active person who

liked to be as busy as possible in spite of my blindness, and that I would not be content to sit back and let someone else do everything for me. There were many things I could still do, including cooking, so why not continue to do these things? I already knew that life was full of uncertainties so I agreed that it would be foolish to lose the ability to look after myself. Now I had a guide dog to help me enjoy life to the full, so why not expand!

• *Love your pet.* A television program featured an 80-year-old stroke victim, delightedly caressing an appealing tabby kitten. "She's mine, and I love her. She's made me the happiest person in the world," the recovering patient declared.

Science is studying the effects of something you've long known—that there's real therapy present when something small and furry lights up your life. Imagine the loneliness inherent in the stroke patient's long, slow comeback. How great to have a funny, naughty puffball scamper into your heart at such a time!

In many communities, Humane Society volunteers deliver small animals to nursing homes or wherever else the elderly reside. They've discovered that a heart-attack victim who returns home to a dog recovers quicker.

"The elderly need to give," a physician stated. "The handicapped need responsibility, and something that requires them to make an effort."

Which animals are best for lonely, handicapped older people? "Soft, furry pets," a Humane Society volunteer replied. "Choose kittens, rabbits, or chinchillas . . . anything soft and cuddly."

A University of Pennsylvania conference on the human/animal bond reported that pets provide an improved quality of life for lonely, elderly, housebound individuals. Pet-therapy programs are popping up in nursing homes, psychiatric hospitals, and prisons. What a delightful Rx for the Super Years!

• *Play is important in your life.* All your life, you'll benefit from play, according to Irwin Rosen, Ph.D., a psychoanalyst who directs the Menninger Foundation's Adult Outpatient Department in Topeka, Kansas. "We need to learn that the development of a sense of playfulness and its appropriate use is a life task, not just a childhood one ... play for self-growth, self-knowledge, replenishment, creativity, joy," he said.

Be ready for play. Help dispel loneliness by allowing yourself to play. Question: If you could choose a toy for yourself, what would it be? Anything—from bolo bat to yo-yo to kazoo—goes. Rx for loneliness: Go fly a kite!

• *Keep loneliness out of your marriage.* Your Super Years can bring you closer and closer to your beloved. These ideas might help:

1. *Write a love letter.* Tell him or her the things you're still too shy to express. Learn some new ways to say, "I appreciate you."

2. *Take a ride or a stroll together.* Share some good, positive feelings for one another. No analysis, no criticism—just *positive* feelings.

3. *Ask questions; continue to know him or her better.* Who was his favorite hero when he was a child? What is his secret ambition? What was the happiest day of his life?

4. *Think up at least three compliments today—and say them!*

5. *Touch him or her in a simple way.* Convey the tenderness you feel. Above all, say, "I love you."

The Super Years offer time and space for affirming one another. Cherish your time together. Cherish the man or woman you chose, and the intimacy you now can afford to nurture.

• *Consider remarriage at any age.* Virginia whispered, "I'm so lonely. I hate living alone." She hesitated, dropped her eyes, then

plunged into the question: "Should I even *think* about remarriage
... at ... at ... *sixty-three?*"

The question came too late, of course. Obviously Virginia *was*
thinking about it! And why not? Why do so many lonely older
people remain unmarried—fearful of what society at large and
their children, in particular, might say?

Measure your own loneliness. Make your own decisions. Everyone else should respect your willingness to do so. Share your
Super Years if you wish!

Help stamp out loneliness. Begin with yourself: really get to
know your Self, and begin to like the person you are. Also, determine *not* to be lonely. "Despondency is ingratitude; hope is God's
worship," Henry Ward Beecher declared.

Learn to laugh (children make great teachers), and find yourself a laughin' place. Or adopt a wiggly pup or a warm kitten, just
to make loneliness impossible.

Invest in your friendships; your grandchildren; your husband
or wife; in new loves, near and far. Reach out. Embrace those
Super Years, and everyone in them!

CHAPTER 12

The Beauty Around You

You need and deserve a *beautiful* home. Everyone does. I believe every person on earth has an idea . . . a dream . . . maybe just a scrap of a picture, tucked away somewhere in his mind. Oh, he may never speak of it, but I believe a home—even an unspoken, mental picture—exists in each human heart.

Corrie ten Boom carried such a picture in her mind. During her World War II imprisonment at the notorious Ravensbruck Prison, Corrie often spoke to her sister Betsie about the bright, clean, flower-filled house they'd buy and share someday.

That day never came. Gallant Betsie died in prison. Corrie, miraculously released, devoted the rest of her life to traveling and speaking all over the world, testifying with power about the God of Love. As she traveled those hundreds of thousands of miles, Corrie ten Boom became known as a "tramp for the Lord." She had no home, but she never let go of the dream.

At last, Corrie stopped—and decided to put down roots in the United States. In flower-filled California, she bought her first home—*at age 84.*

I love that story of a woman who, by faith, carried her dream with her (perhaps in her big, black pocketbook) and never, ever let it go. How precious that house must have seemed to Corrie when she received it!

We need not power or splendor;
Wide hall or lordly dome;
The good, the true, the tender,
These form the wealth of home.

SARAH J. HALE

You, too, need such a house—or perhaps just a loft, a space, a room—the size doesn't matter, but your vision does. You know what pleases your spirit. You will recognize your environment when you see it. And meanwhile, you can carry the picture in your head a bit longer—as long as you need to.

Visualize your desire. Begin to believe you'll have that certain house . . . an airy porch . . . a workshop with a place for everything. . . .

Imagine it mentally, but then sharpen your pencil. Begin to write down exactly what you want, imaging in scrupulous detail. Dr. Norman Vincent Peale, the famous minister, author, and speaker, firmly believes in the power of visualizing yourself *living* in the house. In other words, *don't turn loose your dream.*

Those who know what they want usually stand a better than average chance of attaining it. Those who know *themselves,* who understand their dreams, needs, and desires, acquire faith enough to turn dreams into substance.

Stanley Marcus, former chairman of Neiman-Marcus, emphasized that principle in his book *Stanley Marcus: Quest for the Best.* "Customers . . . should not be bashful in their insistence on the best," he wrote, "for, as Somerset Maugham wrote in *The Mixture as Before:* 'It is a funny thing about life, if you refuse to accept anything but the best you very often get it.' "

The best! *You* know what that means—for it has a well-formed, personal size and shape within your mind. Like you, Daniel A. Poling's father loved his house, and had a clear perception of exactly how it should look. In *Mine Eyes Have Seen,* the minister and editor tells of an episode that took place when his father was past 85 and put a new roof on his house in Portland. Daniel Poling wrote:

> . . . As we surveyed the finished job, he was clearly not pleased. "I made a mistake," he told me. "Those synthetic shingles look all right, but an Oregon house should be covered with clear cedar, and that's what I'll put on next." We discussed other matters for what I believed was a reasonable period, and then I asked, "Father, what's your guarantee on that roof?"
>
> Like a flash came the answer: "Fifteen years—and I know what you're thinking!"

How important to your Super Years will your personal environment become? How conscious of light, space, color, and setting will you be? Do flowers matter a lot, or trees?

Theologian Reinhold Niebuhr once said, "The self is a creature which is in constant dialogue with itself, with its neighbors, and with God." In a spirit of dialogue you might take a few minutes for visualizing your present environment with fresh eyes. Consult with yourself about it. See how well it meets your needs and matches your desires.

You'll be able to grade your home and work environments, then consider the everyday effect they exert on your mental, physical, and emotional life. Consider the following questions, answering each according to the following guide:

Excellent—3

Satisfactory—2

Needs Improving—1

Unsatisfactory—0

Now, on a large piece of paper, write:

MY ENVIRONMENT

How do I like my home, in terms of function?

Do I have sufficient space?

Enough visual beauty?

Do I enjoy the colors around me?

Is there serenity and order?

Is my home warm and cozy?

Does it "entertain" well?

Do I enjoy inviting others there?

Do I have an efficient work environment?

Conducive to my own relaxation and productivity?

Free from irritating noise?

Good air conditioning?

Visually serene?

Does my home environment stimulate me?

Do I have a corner for myself and my activities?

A place to relax?

A spot for a cozy tête-à-tête?

Exercise space?

A garden?

A laughin' place?

Music?

Good lighting?

A good bed?

Now, let's redesign your own space. Pretend you can make any change you desire—large or small. Take a sheet of paper and begin to visualize these changes and mentally make them happen, room by room, in your house.

Mentally walk through your space and order the changes you'd like. Write your desires on paper, as if you were writing a memo which would be followed implicitly. As you write, think in terms of color, function, beauty, joy, self-expression, gaiety, and comfort. Add anything you'd like to each room of your house—flowers, pictures, lights, new carpets, *anything at all.*

List each area of your house, leaving space to write your "directions" concerning that area. Be sure to include:

My bedroom

Guest room

Living room

Dining room

Kitchen

Office

Porches and hallways

Basement or attic

You are a designer. You design the look and feel of your space by the simple addition of a potted plant, or the positioning of a chair. Daily, you and I design our environments, whether we change anything or *not*—for the very *neglect* to change stamps our environment with our tacit okay.

Ever so quietly, we respond to the space in which we live. Do you like your space? Does it reflect your desires? Will you change it? Does it mirror your Self image? Does this space deserve to become part of your Super Years?

You need beauty. You were born beautiful, and set within a world that is forever fair. Your soul responds to loveliness, order, and composition; it thrills to color and harmony.

Your Super Years can contain the great blessing of beauty— beauty within you, beside you, and around you—if you desire and expect it. As Emerson wrote,

> Never lose an opportunity of seeing anything that is beautiful; for beauty is God's handwriting—a wayside sacrament. Welcome it in every fair face, in every fair sky, in every fair flower, and thank God for it as a cup of blessing.

Deeply religious Bernard of Clairvaux said, "What we love we shall grow to resemble."

Carry all the beauty you can, into your Super Years!

CHAPTER 13

Love Yourself

SHE'S short, plump, and matronly, and except for a certain glint in her eye, looks rather undistinguished. Within that well-corseted package, however, resides a gal whose personality packs a real wallop. Nobody ever forgets Frances!

Consider the time she and Arthur boarded ship for a trip to England. Arriving passengers received name tags that read "HELLO! I'm _____"

Frances didn't hesitate. With bold strokes, she penned in her identification: ADORABLE. The "mystery woman" met more new friends than anyone else on that cruise. Whether or not they recall her name, they'll forever remember Frances as *adorable*.

"Every one stamps his own value on himself," Schiller wrote. In fact, we all label ourselves daily. HELLO! I'm: HAPPY. EXCITED. DISPLEASED. AFRAID. TICKLED PINK. (Who are you today?)

The Super Years become increasingly more rewarding as you learn to love your Self. Question: *Do I love myself?* Am I lovable? How do I really feel about *me?* Millions of people suffer from a disease that's quite responsive to proper treatment—a debilitating malady called "low self-worth." Low self-worth produces lifelong, destructive side effects. However, there's a cure for this widespread plague. Rx: Megadoses of straight thinking, common sense, tolerance, forgiveness, and love. (Apply this mixture daily, as needed.)

You can be cured even from self-contempt, self-hatred, and hopelessness. Simply take one or more of the following love capsules, as needed:

You are good. God makes all things good. You are one of His highest creations, marvelously designed and constructed; custom-fitted for your particular time and place in world history.

Take time to appreciate how well made you really are. Think how well you function (most of the time) and what a fine degree of accuracy you exhibit (usually). At your best, you're exquisitely fine tuned. At your worst, you're still the most amazing machine within our universe.

You are good. Get your basic goodness into perspective. Take it into account. Your Super Years can polish that natural, divinely intended goodness to a radiant shine. Respect that fact. Believe *you are good.*

You are worth loving. If you love those things that are good, it follows that you must love yourself. You are a worthwhile person. Even if you dislike your looks, habits, or emotions, you cannot rationally deny the fact of your basic worth. What are your three most valuable characteristics? Are they common to all of us, or singularly yours? Do you take yourself for granted?

You are *tremendously* well worth loving. If you feel less than totally convinced of that fact, try this simple exercise. Ask your marriage partner or other close friend to list five priceless assets you possess, while you list five of his or hers.

Swap lists. Read and study what someone close to you has revealed. Tell the other person how you feel about what he has written.

Jack wrote: *You are guileless. You speak honestly. You possess courage. You know how to give. You are faithful.* As Millie read Jack's list, tears filled her eyes. "Am I really all those things?" she whispered.

"Much more than that," Jack responded. "You only asked me for five."

You are *innately* worthy of deep respect and love. Try to comprehend that overwhelming fact. Recognizing your value will help you with this point.

Take good care of yourself. Are your careless? Tom cut his hand, tore his raincoat, and broke out with poison-ivy blisters— all in the same weekend. Bad luck? Maybe. Or perhaps Tom stopped treating himself as the valuable and irreplaceable person he actually is.

Do you get good marks for self-care? How well do you maintain your body? Your happiness level? Your sleep, rest, and need for good food?

Love yourself enough to take good care of yourself. If you don't presently possess that self-love, simply begin to take the very finest self-maintenance measures in your own behalf. See love and self-respect follow!

Dress well. "Is all this mere trifling?" Maurice Goudeket asks in his autobiography. "No: it is good manners. Good manners require one to show the people around one, and the rest of the world, the least saddening appearance that one can manage.

"I know nothing more moving than some very old married couples who have kept a mutual desire to please and who have therefore by no means let themselves go. And it may well be that they owe their long life to these little daily restraints, this exercise of self-control."

Celebrate yourself! Dress well because you deserve it. Realize that you're worth every moment you spend on your appearance. Your dress reflects your mood, your spirit, your personal statement. Love yourself and dress accordingly.

Hang in there with yourself. The Super Years give you space for self-tolerance, for picking yourself up after yet another fall. Persevere. Try again. Try harder, next time, to achieve whatever you want.

Trust yourself. Your instincts usually pan out. You're worth having faith in, after all, so practice that faith—continually. Above all, *don't* keep yourself on trial.

Give yourself more scope. The Super Years offer you, most likely, much more turning-around room than you've had in the past. With the children raised and gone, your job or profession established, your home largely paid for, your world begins to widen.

Seize the opportunity. Love yourself enough to risk some things. Start a new business, if you desire. Retire early and sail around the world. Or return to college.

"I'm so proud of my wife," Steve boasted. "She raised eight kids and still looks like a million dollars. Now she's working toward her master's degree. I *like* a liberated woman!"

Like yourself and expand that Self when the opportunity arises. You'll *love* the results.

Take stock of the many things you do well. If you'd begin listing the skills you've acquired thus far into your life, you'd soon compile an impressive listing. By the time you reach age fifty, you'll discover you've learned so many skills you literally cannot think of them all.

Beginning with walking and talking, think of all you have learned to do proficiently. Reading, dancing, singing, memorizing, praying, thinking, joking, cooking, bed making, driving a car. . . .

Those are *anybody's* skills. But what about your specialties? Reading a blueprint. Cutting and stitching a dress. Writing a song. Building a house. Making a perfect pound cake.

You do so many things so very well, you should fall in love with yourself all over again!

Stay in touch with your Self. You are someone very important to know. Does your Self know that? Does that Self think of you as a V.I.P.?

If not, get in touch. Think of all the things you could very well like and enjoy about yourself. *Your small waistline and tremendous sense of humor. Your youthful exuberance and age-old wisdom. Your reserved manner, sometimes punctuated by unrestrained joy.* You are a study in contrasts. Your fascinating, multifaceted Self twinkles like a star. Will you *ever* understand all the things you are?

Get in touch with your feelings. *Know* how you feel about controversial issues, household standards, community ventures, family disputes. Practice reviewing your feelings. The Super Years offer time and space to get in touch with every side of you—feelings, thoughts, responses, personality traits.

Explore the inner person. Ask yourself some questions. Do some personal thinking. In short, get in touch with your Self—then, *stay* in touch!

Find some friends of the opposite sex. Love yourself better: that's often what friends of the opposing gender help you to do. Why? There's something about having a sounding board. . . .

The Super Years offer more and better opportunities for you to relate openly and well with others. There's much to be said for all friendships, but especially for men-women friendships. More than a century ago, Florence Nightingale wrote, "The thing needed . . . is these friendships without love between men and women. And if between married men and married women, all the better."

Why? Because it's useful to explore the other side of the mental and emotional coin. As Victor Hugo said, "Men have sight; women insight."

Consider taking more time to converse with buddies of the opposite gender. It's a great way to discover alternate ways of looking at topics, of giving and receiving straightforward, other-viewpoint advice.

Often we can relate to our alter-egos with especially vital, caring honesty. That marvelous, unselfish sort of man-woman synergy enriches both. Suggestion: when your thinking gets stuck, run the idea or question past a person of the other sex. Get a new perspective. It reenforces each of you, even as it opens wide the windows of your mind.

Learn ways to put more love into your life. Jerry cultivates children. "I'll be your friend, ready to help you with your problems," he tells them. "We'll always be friends—forever.

"When you're my age," he continues, "I'll be getting old. It's neat that when I become old you'll be grown up. Then you can help *me* with *my* problems!" Jerry brags that "his kids" keep him continually on his toes. They are endlessly creative, he says, and often wondrously funny. Jerry offers them the sort of dignified caring he'd extend to any adult friend—and they respond in kind.

"When I was four, Mother let me walk next door to visit Miss

Elkins, my first adult friend," Jerry recalled. "She and I talked about everything under the sun. She had a real impact on my life.

"I remember Miss Elkins very well. I hope I'm half as patient, as good about sharing my best thinking with these little friends as she did with me. God bless her; she was *great.*"

Put more love into your life. Remember, your heart is made of elastic. It stretches to encompass endless amounts of love!

Give yourself freedom to grow and change. Love yourself and allow yourself to burst out of old habit patterns. Love yourself enough to quit smoking; quit procrastinating; quit anything that holds you back.

You deserve the freedom to try and the freedom to fail. Offer yourself freedom to *grow*—even (especially) when you fail. Love yourself when you fail. Dust off that bruised ego and treat it tenderly.

Failure is painful; *change* is painful; *growth* very often seems painful, at any stage of life. It takes real self-love to permit a process that first must produce pain before it can produce ultimate triumph.

Revoke all forms of personal bondage. Love yourself enough to break those artificial restraints—smutty films or reading matter, compulsive overeating, unwise spending—that shackle you or deprive you of free choice. Individuals who would never submit voluntarily to wearing handcuffs, for example, will walk around with a cigarette occupying their fingers.

To choose still another example, consider the millions who pop over-the-counter pills. Aspirins, sleep remedies, laxatives, vitamins by the handfuls—even chain coffee-drinking.

Has some such annoying and unnecessary habit got you stymied? Give it up during your Super Years! Don't be handcuffed.

Break out of the bondage you chose for yourself in earlier years. You can do it!

Refuse to choose privation. "Po-mouthin'," as we call it in the South, actually creates poverty. It's a self-fulfilling prophecy wherein individuals actually choose privation (the easy way out) rather than make a real decision. Mindless self-denial strips our lives, robs our initiative, and reduces our standards.

Resolve to say *yes* to yourself more often than you say *no*. Raise your standard of living. Do this confidently, without fear. You can break the most deeply ingrained habits of unnecessary self-denial. You can begin to thrive!

Refuse all undue stress. Super Years—rich with health and well-being, excitement, and fun—cannot coexist with unhealthy stress.

How much do you willingly stress yourself? Have you made overwork a lifelong habit? Do you drive seven hundred miles the first day of your vacation? Have you been President in Perpetuity for several organizations?

If so, consult yourself. You can cure that "glutton for punishment" syndrome, if you wish. Its rewards can include not only chronic fatigue, but irritability, muscle spasms, insomnia, gastric upsets, arthritis, heart disease, and other bad news. Surely you love yourself too much to endure "stress punishment" indefinitely!

Spread beauty around. "Leave things better than you found them," ordered your father and mine. Neatness, order, beauty— these are habits—a way of life.

The Super Years afford us priceless opportunities to foster beauty. We can begin with our Self—body, intellect, emotions— and work forward. Added years can provide added elegance, refinement, and charm. Increase your knowledge and appreciation of beauty. Learn crafts, study music, improve your home, your garden, or your community.

Become more beauty conscious. Become more and more beautiful. It's your choice.

Keep friendships in repair. Miss Layona Glenn, who entered Brazil in 1898 as one of the first Protestant missionaries, established a lifelong habit of devotion to friendships. Of necessity, many of these were conducted by mail. At age 103, she wrote as many as a dozen letters per day and maintained long-distance relationships begun in her youth.

"Some of those early friends died, then their kids took up writing to me," she reported. "After a while those kids died, and now I correspond with their grandkids," Miss Layona explained.

Few of us remain that faithful. Friendships that last a half-century and more are rare. indeed. Invest more in your friendships, and the rewards—precious intimacy and lifelong companionship—unfailingly accrue.

Take stock of your friendships. Decide to make each one something truly special. Love your friends, and love your Self.

Value your ideas. You've hatched dozens and dozens of good ideas during your life. Where did they come from? Where did they go?

If you are an idea person (and you are), perhaps it's time you began to take them more seriously. Keep a notebook and pen at your bedside, then record dreams or ideas that occur at night. *Write them down,* sleep experts advise. Otherwise, your ideas are siphoned off and wasted.

Ask yourself if your ideas usually get pooh-poohed. Do you fight for them? Should you implement some of them?

Simply acting upon your good ideas can raise your abilities, your self-concept, and your chances to prosper throughout your Super Years.

Realize you are a sexual being. You were born that way—very male, or very female. Like other valuable physical, mental, and emotional attributes, your sexuality is designed to last your entire lifetime. It pervades your personality—your face, your walk, your clothing choices, your laugh, your scent, your gestures. None of these is random.

Listen more to the distinctly sexual side of your Self. Enjoy your masculinity or femininity. Enhance it and allow it to flower. Determine to enjoy your special sexual nature all the days of your life.

Let the past go. The Super Years are *now,* not then. As Christian Bovee wrote, "The past is the sepulchre of our dead emotions."

Place your hand on your heart. Feel the exciting reality of that steady, healthy beat. Feel the current of your life. It represents *now.* The past—particularly past griefs, mistakes, or bitterness—can slow or even clog that current.

Let the past go. Begin to cherish today!

God believes in you. He created you to do great exploits. He gives you (and all mankind) dominion over this vast earth and everything in it.

Faith in *you?* Undeniably. Your faith in *Him?* That "faith as a grain of mustard seed" can move mountains, Jesus said. If you would move mountains, foster that faith.

"All I have seen teaches me to trust the Creator for all I have not seen," Emerson wrote.

God believes in you. He made you good, worth loving and infinite care. You deserve to be adorned, to be trusted, to be given more scope. You've learned to do many things very well. God wants you to stay in touch with yourself.

CHAPTER 14

Give Yourself Away

It's totally possible for you, me, and anyone else in the world to enjoy the Super Years this book describes—if we'll obey one simple imperative: *We must learn to give ourselves away.*

All highly successful people know that *giving generates power.* In fact, there can *be* no real success apart from giving. Famous ballet dancers, trial lawyers, preachers, football stars, and the many, many others who pour their brains, talents, and hearts into their professions, model this truth before us. Often these people seem to *live* in order to *give.*

"For each hour I perform, I've practiced perhaps one thousand hours," a French horn symphonic player told his son. "I stay prepared to give everything I've got."

The musician *intends* to give himself away. As you and I plan for our Super Years, we can adopt the same stance. Even though my life might seem far less practiced than his, infinitely less well fine tuned, I, like the musician, can benefit from the power-packed principles behind consistent, continuous giving.

Trouble is, too many of us believe we have little or nothing of importance to offer others. I hope this chapter will explode that fallacy. Even a moment of serious thought should convince us that nobody ever becomes so poor, so bankrupt, that he literally has nothing left to give. By contrast, he or she who proffers the "widow's mite" discovers that giving generates abundant life. Study the people around you who give the most, and you'll also observe that they seem to receive far more from life than most of us do. It's a law of nature: The more we give, the more we receive.

Learn to give yourself away. To start, let's consider the dictionary definition of *gift:*

> *Something that is bestowed voluntarily and without compensation; a present. The act, right, or power of giving. A talent, endowment, aptitude, or bent.*

Your life by now has lavished you with riches and endowments. Like all of us, you inherited some gifts, gained others by your own efforts, and a few appeared through blessed serendipity or happenstance.

You're all set to give yourself away. You're prepared to seize the adventure of all adventures: the pouring of yourself and your gifts into the treasury. You realize, as Lessing did, that "it is the will, and not the gift that makes the giver."

How to begin? Let's try what I call the *3-D* approach:

1. **Define** your gifts.

2. **Develop** your gifts.

3. **Decide** to become a lifelong giver.

Those three simple steps lead to the shining, enduring platform beneath your Super Years. You soon discover you need no special talents, strength, or wealth to emulate those brilliant, vital, and glittering persons—the rarest and most special people—who give themselves unstintingly to the world.

Like them, you can become expert at giving. You can become habituated to giving. You'll almost certainly become tangibly and intangibly wealthy through giving, as you begin to utilize the power generated by the law of continuing generosity—an unseen force that can neither be assessed nor measured. Quite simply, it's awesome. And it's readily available to you.

Think. What gifts will you develop during your Super Years? What special powers do you possess? What is there about yourself you can begin to foster, nurture, and enjoy?

Perhaps in the past you considered your own giftedness too slight to bother about. Or perhaps you *know* you hide your light (your talents for art, organization, public speaking, compassionate outreach, your gift for anything at all) under a bushel. Whatever the case, you can use the *3-D* approach.

Define your gifts. Begin with the simple recognition that you probably take for granted most of your giftedness and much about yourself that's unique. It's not easy to take an objective look at one's attributes, but do it anyhow. Remember, the outcome of this exercise should excite (and even *ennoble*) you, as you discover old and new personal treasures with which to bless others.

How, exactly, can you define your gifts? How to recognize your own latent talents? There are several ways to begin that personal search, but the best place to start might be with *desire*. Reread chapter 4 with this question in mind: *Which of my deep personal desires tie in directly with my special giftedness?*

There's an easy and graphic way you can answer such questions (not an answer, actually, but a thought process that could begin today and continue forever). Divide a large sheet of paper into three columns. Write:

1. I Want to *Be* . . .

2. I Want to *Do* . . .

3. I Want to *Own* . . .

Jot your thoughts beneath the appropriate headings as rapidly as they come to mind. Don't stop to think, just write. You'll be surprised at what emerges.

Then take another large sheet. At the top, write "My Gifts." List your accomplishments, beginning with walking, talking, singing, and other such fundamental functions. These are *gifts?* you ask. Of course! Try getting along without speech, sight, or a sense of smell.

As you write, begin to appreciate exactly how talented and well trained you've become. Driving a car: *Millions of people in this world could envy you that skill.* Reading: *Any illiterate man or woman would love to have such abilities!* Cooking: *Not only can you recognize dozens of foodstuffs, herbs, and condiments, you know how to use them. American supermarkets and food know-how would bewilder residents of this world's other six continents. Never take such skills for granted.*

You get the picture. Leave your lists where you can add to them regularly. You'll soon feel elated and amazed at what you see. You are gifted, talented, and superbly trained: it's all there in black and white! Obviously you're ready to give yourself away.

At that point, it's important to realize that *you begin exactly where you are.* Even without exceptional training, expensive tuition, or ponderous exercise, life by now has showered you with gifts beyond measure. You can relate to a widow who emerged on the American art scene a generation ago—a spare, simple housewife, who eventually astounded millions with her acute powers of observation.

Anna Mary Robertson Moses was past sixty when she picked up a brush and began to paint her memories of idyllic times and places in our national scene. Untrained, she never pretended to education she didn't possess. Throughout her sixties, seventies, eighties, nineties, and into her centennial year, Grandma Moses enchanted and enriched art critics and ordinary folk alike.

Special gifts? You can argue that Grandma Moses had them, or you can insist that she did not. That's really not the question. The point is, her decision to give herself away has enlarged us all.

Even had Grandma Moses never painted a lick, however, she possessed a God-given ability to see and share the sort of things that stir and touch us. Imagine yourself writing about everyday life, as she did in *Grandma Moses: My Life's History* (edited by Otto Kallir):

In the springtime of life there is plenty to do. Oh, those damp snowy days, early in spring, when we loved to go to the woods, and look for the first bloom of the trailing arbutus, which sometimes blooms beneath the snow, or gather the pussy willows. Feeling nearer to God's intentions, nearer to nature. Where in some respect, we are free, where there is beauty and tranquility, where we sometimes long to be, quiet and undisturbed, free from the hubbub of life.

Haying time on the farm, when they gather the grain, fruit and berries of all description, and the little folks gather the eggs. When the church picnic comes, and the children can have all the cake and lemonade they want, watermelon and peanuts, what a wonderful treat!

And the fall of the year, and there are many odd jobs to attend to, food to be stored away for the coming cold weather, the ground to be plowed for rye and other crops before it is frozen hard. Ditches to dig. Poultry to sell and house.

Thanksgiving, in some homes there will be rejoicing, in others there will be sorrow. But we, that can give thanks, should, there is so much to be thankful for, and praise God for all blessings, and the abundance of all things.

And then wintertime! When zero stands at 25 or 30, when we cannot deny the pleasure of skating till we have bumped heads, and bleedy noses, and the ice is like glass. Oh what joy and pleasure as we get together, to go for the Christmas tree, what aircastles we build as we slide down the hill, who can rebuild what we see on that Christmas tree.

Oh, those days of childhood!

Like Grandma Moses, you have so much to give! Begin to define your gifts. Have confidence in what you know. Begin to give yourself away.

Develop your gifts. "Taste and quality can be self-taught," declared Stanley Marcus, former chairman of Neiman-Marcus. Beyond that teaching, though, lies a vitally important schooling common to every genius you've ever admired: persistency. *You can teach yourself to persist.* Through simply becoming persistent, you can develop your gifts. Indeed, there's no other way to do so!

Take a look at your own impressive list of personal gifts. Which do you consider your best strengths? How much did you *persist* in order to ski, play the piano, or use hand tools? Which lesser gifts on your list could you maximize through a simple decision to persist?

George Washington Carver, towering scientist, educator, and humanitarian, was born during America's Civil War into a world that could offer virtually no encouragement toward fostering his considerable talents. Lawrence Elliott's book *George Washington Carver: The Man Who Overcame* records the incredible exploits Carver derived from sheer persistence. Born black, choosing to cast his lot with other blacks in the rural South; struggling to educate himself and others during the bleak and hungry years of postwar reconstruction; it's incredible to imagine Carver gaining even a toehold on life, despite his genius.

George Washington Carver, by dint of assiduous self-directed work and study, became a giant in American science, even as he helped develop a struggling black college in rural, backwoods Alabama. At Tuskegee Institute, the rustic school which would become world-famous through his influence, Carver studied the lowly peanut. Before he died, the homely "goober pea" had more than three hundred industrial uses!

"The peanut, Carver had shown, could provide virtually everything man needed to sustain life," Elliott wrote.

Persistency! Simple, dogged work enabled the amazing George Washington Carver to turn peanuts into mayonnaise, instant coffee, cheese, chili sauce, shampoo, bleach, axle grease, linoleum, metal polish, wood stains, adhesives, plastics and wallboard, according to his biographer, who wrote:

> More than a scientist and a "doctor of plants," Carver was a man of many talents. He toured as a pianist to raise money for the Institute . . . wheeled a wagon and a mule through impoverished, isolated farm lands to demonstrate the techniques of raising, improving and conserving foods. At the Institute he earned money to enlarge its acreage, designed a new building and landscaped its campus.
>
> He won the friendship of three presidents—Theodore Roosevelt, Calvin Coolidge and Franklin D. Roosevelt . . . spent three weeks teaching the Crown Prince of Sweden agricultural

methods ... corresponded with Gandhi, offering him food conservation ideas to help his starving peoples ... and exchanged periodic visits with his friend Henry Ford.

Yes, develop your gifts. Like Dr. Carver, you can learn to continue feeding and exercising your talents. You do not require genius to learn persistency. However, every genius has learned to persist.

Decide to become a giver. In *Priceless Gifts: How to Give the Best to Those You Love,* author and clinical psychologist Dr. Daniel A. Sugarman says our capacity for happiness is only as great as our ability to give and express love. Dr. Sugarman listed twelve super highways toward those feelings:

1. The gift of time

2. The gift of a good example

3. The gift of acceptance

4. The gift of seeing the best in people

5. The gift of privacy

6. The gift of self-esteem

7. The gift of giving up a bad habit

8. The gift of self-disclosure

9. The gift of helping someone learn something new

10. The gift of really listening

11. The gift of fun

12. The gift of letting others give to you

As the psychologist observes, all twelve of those "gifts" are like two-way streets. You receive by giving. What's more, you'll never become too old to give, or too feeble, or too poor.

Lydia Niebuhr, mother of the noted theologian Reinhold Niebuhr, personified the giver of truly precious gifts, the gifts of Self. "Even in her mid-eighties, she was a Pied Piper to the children on the McCormick Seminary Campus who visited her several times a week to paint and carve, to sew and make designs out of stained glass, to cook and eat," Niebuhr's biographer recounted. *Lydia Niebuhr knew how to give herself away.*

Stanley Marcus echoes that philosophy. "Public service is the rental price you pay for your space on earth," he says. *He demonstrates the power of giving oneself away.*

Deborah Szekely, founder of the Golden Door health spa, California civic leader and ardent champion of volunteerism, was asked why she wanted to run for Congress. "The Japanese divide life into three parts," she explained. "The first third is growing up and getting an education; the second is marriage and money; the third is achieving dreams. I'm sixty years old, this is the third part of my life and I dream of using in Congress some of the skills I've developed in my volunteer work and in operating my business."

Mrs. Szekely gives herself away.

As Lawrence Elliott wrote about George Washington Carver:

He urged students to think hard about what they had to give to others. Money is not man's most important asset. Peter had no money to give to the poor cripple, so he offered courage and hope. They, too, must learn to give what they had—their talent, their friendship, a cheering word. All the great men of history, from Jesus to Dr. [Booker T.] Washington, had this sainted sense of giving.

Decide to give. Without such decision, there could be no Grandma Moses, no George Washington Carver, no Lydia Niebuhr, or Deborah Szekely. How much genius dies and is buried because its possessor feels too old, too uneducated, too black, too ignorant, too foreign, too poor? Ask yourself about your own genius. Make a decision to give yourself away!

Define your gifts. Develop your gifts. Decide to give. That's the *3-D* approach to life beyond your wildest dreams! *Learn to give yourself away.* In so doing, you give yourself a Way . . . a Way outside and beyond . . . a Way that utterly transcends your ordinary paths . . . a Way that's passionate, selfless, and straight to the heart of your Super Years.

CHAPTER 15

Potpourri

(A Few Grateful Thoughts)

Each life speaks its own language. *Gratitude. Praise. Thanksgiving. Appreciation. Enthusiasm. Faith.* My person, my face, my heart—are they easy to read? Gratitude needs no translator; it speaks for itself.

Let's be grateful! Keep books on our blessings. This year is a Super Year: *pass it on!*

What's ahead? More Super Years! We write our own tickets, you know. Enter in with enthusiasm, go with gratitude, and *bon voyage.* Be grateful for the trip.

Celebrate life. Despite illness, trials, and mistakes, you prevail. *"In all these things we are more than conquerors. . ."* (Romans 8:37). Those words are true; we can be grateful.

How much you know about life! So many lessons already learned . . . such valuable one-time-only mistakes experienced . . . pools of tragedy and joy . . . pockets of foolishness . . . by now, you know, you've seen 'most everything. Be grateful!

Smiles. Even the not-so-Super Years have their share of smiles. Sweet moments, funny mishaps, small jokes on ourselves; these pop up even at the worst of times, like wild flowers blooming between cracks in the sidewalk. Be grateful for smiles.

He who anticipates, very often wins. "Expect a miracle," Oral Roberts says. And why not? Miracles happen; especially when it seems we must search for even the merest shreds of desperate belief. (". . . help thou my unbelief.")

Belief *is* the miracle, at times. Be grateful that your pilot light never gets snuffed out.

ATTITUDE CHANGES AHEAD. Perhaps we should post an interior traffic sign alerting us to such detours. Be grateful we *can* change our attitudes. Otherwise, we'd crash.

Intentionally or not, we create our individual Life's Alphabet, a hodge-podge compendium in which we believe, certain words which, like big brass keys, open special areas of faith within us.

We add and subtract at will, of course, according to personal experience. Here's a bit of my present alphabet, lovingly aimed toward the Super Years and always, of course, subject to expansion.

A. **Appreciate**—"To feel exquisitely is the lot of very many; but to appreciate belongs to the few. Only one or two, here and there, have the blended passion and understanding which, in its essence, constitutes worship."

ELIZABETH S. SHEPPARD

B. **Bestow**—"I never knew a child of God being bankrupted by his benevolence. What we keep we may lose, but what we give to Christ we are sure to keep."

T. L. CUYLER

C. **Cheer**—"What sunshine is to flowers, smiles are to humanity. They are but trifles, to be sure; but, scattered along life's pathway, the good they do is inconceivable.

"A cheerful temper joined with innocence will make beauty attractive, knowledge delightful, and wit good-natured. It will lighten sickness, poverty, and affliction; convert ignorance into an amiable simplicity, and render deformity itself agreeable."

JOSEPH ADDISON

"Cheerfulness is a friend to grace; it puts the heart in tune to praise God, and so honors religion by proclaiming to the world that we serve a good master. Be serious, yet cheerful. Rejoice in the Lord always."

WATSON

D **Discipline**—"A man in old age is like a sword in a show window. Men that look upon the perfect blade do not imagine the process by which it was completed. Man is a sword; daily life is the workshop; and God is the artificer; and those cares which beat upon the anvil, the inscription on the hilt—those are the very things that fashion the man."

HENRY WARD BEECHER

"No pain, no palm; no thorns, no crown; no gall, no glory; no cross, no crown."

WILLIAM PENN

E **Encourage**—"I believe that any man's life will be filled with constant and unexpected encouragement, if he makes up his mind to do his level best each day, and as nearly as possible reaching the high-water mark of pure and useful living."

BOOKER T. WASHINGTON

F **Face Forward**—"Your salvation is in your own hands; in the stubbornness of your minds, the tenacity of your hearts, and such blessings as God, sorely tried by His children, shall give us."

ADLAI STEVENSON

G **Give**—"Serving God with our little, is the way to make it more; and we must never think that wasted with which God is honored, or men are blest."

JOHN HALL

"The heart of the giver makes the gift dear and precious."

MARTIN LUTHER

H **Hope**—"You cannot put a great hope into a small soul."

J. L. JONES

I **Imagine**—"The soul without imagination is what an observatory would be without a telescope."

HENRY WARD BEECHER

J **Joy**—"We ask God to forgive us for our evil thoughts and evil temper, but rarely, if ever, ask Him to forgive us for our sadness."

R. W. DALE

K **Know**—"The end of all learning is to know God, and out of that knowledge to love and imitate Him."

JOHN MILTON

L **Laugh**—"A good laugh is like sunshine in a house."

WILLIAM THACKERAY

M **Mean Business**—"Energy will do anything that can be done in this world; and no talents, no circumstances, no opportunities will make a two-legged animal a man without it."

GOETHE

N **Nurture**—"God could not be everywhere, and therefore He made mothers."

Jewish Proverb

O **Optimize**—"Nothing ages like laziness."

EDWARD BULWER-LYTTON

P **Persevere**—"Every noble work is at first impossible."

THOMAS CARLYLE

Q **Quiet**—"The heart that is to be filled to the brim with holy joy must be held still."

GEORGE BOWES

R **Receive**—"There never was a person who did anything worth doing that did not receive more than he gave."

HENRY WARD BEECHER

S **Succeed**—"The surest way not to fail is to determine to succeed."

RICHARD SHERIDAN

T **Teach**—"Thoroughly to teach another is the best way to learn for yourself."

TRYON EDWARDS

U **Upgrade**—"A large part of virtue consists in good habits."

WILLIAM PALEY

V **Venture**—"Trust God for great things; with your five loaves and two fishes, He will show you a way to feed thousands."

HORACE BUSHNELL

W **Work**—"Concentration is my motto—first honesty, then industry, then concentration."

ANDREW CARNEGIE

X **X-ray** your heart and your life. See yourself truly, and become your own friend.

Y **Yield**—Lord, help me read the road signs. I'm tired of these head-on collisions!

Z **Zoom** into your Super Years with faith, confidence, and joy. I have eagle's wings; am I willing to fly?

Collect wisdom, collect gratitude, to ornament your Super Years. For example, these words from Grandma Moses, written after her ninetieth year:

> I felt older when I was sixteen than I ever did since. I was old and sedate when I left . . . I suppose it was the life I led, I had to be so lady-like. Even now I am not old, I never think of it, yet I am a grandmother to eleven grandchildren, I also have seventeen great-grandchildren, that's a plenty!

And like Grandma Moses, may I write:

> I have written my life in small sketches, a little today, a little yesterday, as I thought of it; as I remembered all the things from childhood on through the years—good ones and unpleasant ones, that is how they come, and that is how we have to take them.
>
> I look back on my life like a good day's work; it was done, and I feel satisfied with it. I was happy and contented; I knew nothing better and made the best out of what life offered. And life is what we make it—always has been—always will be.

Super Years? I'll buy Grandma Moses' wise portrait. "Life is what we make it." Super Years? Totally available to you and me, and that's a promise! Be especially grateful for that promise, for Jesus gave it when He said in Luke 17:21:

> . . . the kingdom of God is within you.

Charlotte Hale's seminars, including "The Super Years," are offered to community, institutional, and corporate groups. For more information, please call or write:

Charlotte Hale
2290 F Dunwoody Crossing
Atlanta, Georgia 30338
(404) 457-4443